PRAISE FOR GUIDED MATH AMPED

Tunstall's knowledge of the teacher experience coupled with her expertise in building upon the conceptual knowledge that each individual student brings to the classroom have the potential to change the trajectory of learners of math. Most educators have come to realize that the magic happens at the teacher table or during small-group instruction. If that's the case, *Guided Math AMPED* is the spell book.

—Jennifer Salyards, MEd, principal,
Chamberlin Elementary, Stephenville ISD

Guided Math AMPED provides educators with a practical framework for enhancing math instruction in a way that provides research-based practices, differentiated instruction, and fun, all while strengthening relationships with students and developing math mindsets. No matter your experience or tenure in education, *Guided Math AMPED* will give you tips and tricks to implement in your classroom. I personally flipped my classroom and saw the results firsthand—scores increased, but my students' confidence as budding mathematicians is what made me a believer.

—Matt Beres, district administrator, Wooster, OH

Guided math is one of the best things you can implement in your classroom, and Reagan Tunstall is the best to learn from, thanks to her perfect framework and step-by-step instructions. She has thought through every potential roadblock and offers concise solutions because she's experienced it all in her own classroom.

—Halee Sikorski, educator, A Latte Learning

Guided Math AMPED provides practical steps teachers can quickly put to use in their classroom that will impact student understanding of mathematical concepts. The clarity that Reagan provides for each component of guided math (warm-up, mini-lesson, guided groups and stations, and lesson reflection) will allow teachers to feel success and flourish in mathematics instruction.

—Kim Johnston, coordinator of mathematics, Midway ISD

Don't you dare let another teacher borrow this book . . . you may never get it back!

From the first page to the end, this book is filled with practical ideas and guidelines guaranteed to take your guided math block to the next level. Reagan covers it all—making it work in any classroom, handling the management to keep it effective, and guiding you through every aspect of implementation.

—**Lori McDonald, MEd,** retired educator

Reagan has the uncanny ability to make you feel like you can conquer the Math Mountain. This book (like her sessions) is filled with everything an educator needs to get started and dig deep!

—**Vera Ahiyya**, educator

Guided math is all about student engagement; it's about learning together. Guided math encourages students to collaborate and actively participate in their own learning and facilitates the learning process for other students in the group. It is differentiation at its best.

—**Dr. Anita Danaher, EdD,** district administration, Calallen ISD

GUIDED MATH AMPED

GUIDED MATH
AMPED

FIVE STEPS TO YOUR
BEST MATH BLOCK

REAGAN TUNSTALL

Guided Math AMPED: Five Steps to Your Best Math Block
© 2021 Reagan Tunstall

This book is available at special discounts when purchased in quantity for use in educational purposes or as premiums, promotions, or fundraisers. For inquiries and details, contact the publisher at books@daveburgessconsulting.com.

Published by Dave Burgess Consulting, Inc.
San Diego, CA
DaveBurgessConsulting.com

Library of Congress Control Number: 2021931005
Paperback ISBN: 978-1-951600-76-1
Ebook ISBN: 978-1-951600-77-8

Cover design by Kapo Ng
Interior design by Liz Schreiter
Editing and production by Reading List Editorial: readinglisteditorial.com

FOR KRISTINA

*The think to my tank, the Wi-Fi to my computer,
the polish to my ideas, the design to my Times New Roman,
the order to my chaos. Thank you for walking with me through
this journey, reminding me of my own math discoveries,
stories, and research, and selflessly giving me your own.*

FOR MY MOM

*The first teacher who pushed the boundaries of classroom
design and creativity, modeled how one captivates and
orchestrates a roomful of students, and shared a genuine
love for the art of a perfect lesson plan.*

FOR MY FAMILY

*For my husband, Tony, and our children, Morgan and Tanner,
for continuously flexing your math muscles in an effort to
diminish mine. PS I wrote a book about math.*

CONTENTS

INTRODUCTION

What if I told you that your math block could be your favorite part of the day? Your excitement could build to teach lessons in new ways, and your students could be begging for math and cheering when you start the math block. This transformation is not only possible, it's easier to realize than you imagine!

When I initially began teaching math, the structure known as "guided math" was not a known or popular teaching format. Whole-group instruction with an emphasis on procedural math thinking was the norm, and I, like the rest of my colleagues, stood at the front of the room, imparting my wisdom as the expert mathematician. Like you, I had the best of intentions, but ultimately all I did was implement a complicated formula that resulted in frustration, a lack of engagement, and burnout for both teachers and students.

For me, the moment I decided I had to make a change happened over two decades ago when I was struck with overwhelming teacher guilt while watching my class silently write my "wise" procedures and answers on their papers while never discussing, exploring, or internalizing the math themselves. This had been my own experience as a student, and much to my dismay, I saw I was merely continuing this pattern. I realized I was simply reinforcing the idea that math was stagnant memorization and not what math ought to be: exciting, engaging, and empowering.

I suspect you, too, have had such a moment, which is why you're holding this book in your hands. Like me, you've been faced with a decision: stay in a comfortable pattern of content delivery because it is familiar (albeit flawed) or find a better way to reach students who have a need to learn differently. When we create change, it's also possible that we create discomfort. But I can confidently tell you you're already part of the way to conquering that discomfort by having found this book.

It was after my realization that my joy for math exploration and discovery was not translating to my students that I began my journey to this new way of running a math block. Unfortunately, that epiphany occurred back in the "dark ages" of teaching before the internet: no email, no computers, no wealth of information right at our fingertips. We received information by pulling paper memos out of our teacher boxes. New learning models and best practices were taught in education workshops or read about in education journals. We couldn't run to Google to grab the latest article on a topic or have a book delivered in just a couple of days from Amazon.

Heading to the library, I researched what limited information I could find on the topic of collaborative math instruction. I began with books explaining small-group learning structures and math exploration. I took small steps and began slowly incorporating the various components of a guided math classroom in the late nineties and early 2000s. Eventually, I gravitated to a four-part structure consisting of the following sections:

- The Warm-Up
- The Mini-Lesson

- Small Groups and Workstations
- The Lesson Reflection

After my initial implementation of the guided math structure, I noticed the undeniable impact it was having on both my students and my teaching practices in comparison to a traditional math block. As a result, I became a die-hard supporter, researcher, and ultimately advocate for this guided math model. Nowadays, I am truly honored to be able to mentor and lead schools and districts to implement guided math practices.

Before we dive into the actual substance of the guided math model, it's worth covering some of the major challenges and benefits that come from amplifying your math block. At the outset, there are a few major issues to consider so you can take the plunge into guided math intentionally and with your eyes open.

GET COMFORTABLE WITH BEING UNCOMFORTABLE

There are no two ways about it: implementing guided math is going to feel uncomfortable at times. When you first attempt to amp up your math block, some interventions are going to short-circuit and some realizations are going to come as a bit of a shock.

In my twenty-two years in education, I have continued to research the ins and outs of guided math through countless resources while simultaneously applying them to my own classroom. As an early adopter of the guided math format, I can honestly say I have taken my students on a journey through many components, structures, and practices—some successfully, and others most definitely the opposite! As I look back, though, the most significant, impactful, and positive changes came out of my unsuccessful moments. Those are the moments that pushed me to find a better way, and you are the beneficiary of my mistakes. In this book I am going to share two decades worth of insights.

At first, I believed if teachers knew the components and purpose of guided math and implemented it, then incredible instruction would be the result. Because I had a profound love for the difference guided math was making in my own classroom, I assumed this would be the case for others. What I found is that each teacher creates and carries out a guided math structure differently. Sometimes I would visit a classroom and be blown away by the results of guided math, and other times I was left scratching my head at how, even with the correct structure in place, things could be so ineffective. Through my years of implementation and mentorship, I began to lean in and take a closer look at each guided math component, students' behaviors within it, and the resulting outcomes.

There's a larger lesson to be taken from my experience, too: while we have a tendency to focus on the structure and components of guided math, the actual impact comes from the small moments that are carried out daily inside the classroom *within* those components. As we discover the power in these small moments, we can learn how best to amplify the impact of our math block. This book is devoted to helping you create those moments for all of your students.

This book is about the discoveries and insights we find by taking a closer look at guided math when just running through the components of guided math isn't enough. This book will explain the guided math structure, but more importantly, it will uncover some common patterns, pitfalls, and moments with the potential for greatness in the guided math classroom. We will learn how to make impactful adjustments together, creating what I call an AMPED math block.

TEACHING GUIDED MATH *YOUR* WAY

Before we jump right into the action plan to amplify our math block, it is essential to know that each teacher will have a unique journey with guided math. Teaching is unique from room to room because of the many varied factors within. Although my philosophy and general teaching beliefs may be similar each year, I encounter unique situations that require different techniques and approaches, and the same will be true for you. Just when you think you have it all figured out, your current system of practice will get upended by the circumstances and challenges of today's classroom. Don't fret! The ineffective teaching practices I highlight are more often than not drawn from my very own experience, and I'll offer tips for avoiding them.

No judgment toward teachers will be found in this book. The assumption here is that we are doing our best to be as effective as we know how. We all have top-of-the-mountain years and then depth-of-the-lowest-valley years. The principles in this book can help guide you through those situations. As you think about the changes you want to make and discomfort begins to rear its head, look into the eyes of your students, sit where they sit in the room, look around and view the day from their perspective. Anytime I am struggling with something in my classroom that I cannot quickly solve, I take these steps. The best part is that as I begin to find the solution, I become empowered, excited, and refreshed! My discomfort shifts to excitement.

It's also important to note at the outset that guided math is not defined by following a curriculum. Instead, guided math is a framework we put into place that allows us to meet with students for targeted instruction. The guided math structure is just that: a structure, a framework for creating the math block of our dreams. The components of guided math are simply a sequence of events for how to run the math block. We will transform this structure into our best math block using intentional placement of instruction, explicit roles in learning, and authentic feedback.

My own understanding of the guided math components happened over time. I organically started components under the umbrella of guided math before knowing I was implementing an existing structure. Through the years, I have found articles, read books, and most importantly listened, watched, and adjusted to the needs of my students. I did not create this structure all in one pivotal day because of something I read or learned. Implementation of the guided math structure and components has been a journey through two decades fueled by my desire to be better at math instruction. It's the result of wanting to create empowered mathematicians.

THE TIME QUESTION

As you consider guided math, amplifying your math block is going to seem like an incredible commitment, especially in terms of time. However, it's important to take a step back and realize that guided math, in the long run, is much more time-effective than traditional math education. This is worth discussing a bit more.

I don't think I have ever done a professional development session without the topic of time coming up as a common pain point. Across the nation, teachers feel stressed for time in relation to content mastery. For this reason, the guided math structure is often avoided. Teachers who haven't had success in the structure, or who haven't tried it out, tend to worry that they won't have enough time with students to bring them to mastery. This is an understandable concern, and I know that teachers are always looking out for students' best interests. The great news is that mini-lessons and small groups allow for complete pedagogical freedom. Regardless of your curriculum, the advantage of this flexible structure is its effectiveness.

My favorite thing about the guided math structure is the impact it can have over the course of many small moments. Let's consider for a moment the format we personally crave for instruction. Consider, for example, when your phone has an issue and isn't working correctly or has a new function that you have never been able to figure out. How would you like to get help? By attending a lecture about the functions of phones or getting face-to-face with someone who can help you with your specific issue? Hello, Apple Store.

Even as we run to YouTube for a quick answer to a household problem or for homework help with our own children, we find ourselves scrolling through a twelve-minute video to get to the instructional point we need. In a classroom setting, we have the power to position the learning for impact. Sometimes we just need to restructure our time in order to do so.

EFFECTIVE IMPACT

In both big and small ways, guided math has the potential to electrify not just your entire classroom but also the experiences of individual students. In fact, that sense of scalability is one of the chief benefits of guided math.

When we teach only in the whole group, we miss impactful learning opportunities that would skyrocket growth and understanding. We need whole-group time to conceptualize and bring everyone to the same enduring understandings. But we also want to have time for students to show us their understanding and specific needs related to that content. Think about how to position the learning for impact. For whole-group lessons, that means get in, teach explicitly, then get out. In guided math terms, this is the mini-lesson component. Then you'd want students to come to you in teacher-led small groups for the specific part of the teaching they need. After that, you'd want to set them free to work independently in structured settings, which is the workstation component.

Often teachers don't feel like there's enough time to incorporate small groups. But if you have a fifteen-minute whole group followed up with ten- or fifteen-minute small-group moments with your students, you will be surprised how many students you can see in a class period. The impact of those focused moments with you is of far greater value for your learners than sitting through a whole-group lesson that isn't addressing the issue they have in the learning.

I also challenge you to have a consistent schedule in which students see you daily, or at least every other day. Don't let them choose to come for help only when they are struggling. Typically, this approach results in teachers either sitting at empty, small-group desks or having a line around the room. These approaches create so much wasted time. Instead, get to know students' everyday math minds through a scheduled time with you. Watch them work through the allotted problems on the current skills, then elevate and expand on what you see. Not only will this direct, consistent approach impact student learning but it will also impact how you teach to students' exact needs.

Underlying consistency in close proximity "face time" with every student will pay off and make all of the difference, just like ten minutes with an expert at the Apple Store regarding your exact problem solves the issue, while an hour-long lesson that's not targeted to your needs does not. Dare I say, daily instruction that doesn't hit a student's learning needs actually creates a negative space where the learning should be.

ADDRESSING LEARNING NEEDS VERSUS COVERING CONTENT

Guided math doesn't just mean reorganizing your math block; it also gives you an opportunity to approach math instruction with a renewed sense of perspective and purpose. In today's classrooms the instructional needs and developmental levels of our students are highly varied, and the conventional math whole-group model has been shown to be less effective. In contrast to the rigid, one-size-fits-all approach of conventional whole-group instruction, guided math allows us the ability to structure our math block to support student learning in risk-free, small-group instruction.

When students say, "I am not good at math," could this actually mean, "My needs for math understanding have not been met and have snowballed over time so that I don't think I will ever truly understand and be confident in my problem-solving"? Each day that a student sits through teaching that doesn't address their particular issue or missing skill, that student is increasingly likely to experience negative feelings and anxieties about math. A face-to-face meeting that involves asking "What can we work on today?" could make all of the difference.

Guided math allows us to be purposeful in addressing learning needs and frees us from the imperative of simply covering content. Generally speaking, educators are rule followers. When given an adopted resource and training on said resource, we then follow the resource as the guide. This model can be helpful in the first year of teaching or in a new grade level as we are establishing an instructional plan and layout for the year from scratch, but the true content we should be concerned with covering is not the resource itself but the math standards for our grade level and the prerequisite skills leading up to our grade level.

You are the content expert; never let a resource drive your instruction. Instead, let your students' math needs drive instruction as you use the resource to address an exact need. How are students reacting to the current objective? Should you enrich the skill, or do they require some foundational skills? Could three problems from the entire lesson actually pinpoint the need? How else can you make little changes to better meet students' needs?

Through the use of small, impactful moments within the guided math structure, we amplify math instruction. When we address the specific areas of concern for our students, we create empowered, confident mathematicians. Creating a systematic way to see every student for a few minutes in a small-group setting, either daily or every other day, allows us to teach new material and specifically help students exactly where needed. Rather than spending our crucial classroom time teaching a whole-group lesson aimed at the middle- to high-achieving student, guided math exposes all students to a new concept, strategy, or procedure in a mini-lesson followed by a small-group lesson to practice and apply the skill in close proximity. Teacher-led small groups allow us to see students work through the content, discuss math thinking, and evaluate how to advance or remediate specific needs.

THE ORGANIZATION OF GUIDED MATH AMPED

I take no credit in offering this guided math structure or its components. My role has been in the implementation of these instructional practices and components with the students I am blessed to work with. As I share my knowledge with you, it comes from the instructional heart of teaching. My gift is in sharing the application of these structures and components. My aim is to show you how these effective math practices *really work* in a classroom and with living, breathing students of all grade levels, backgrounds, and ability levels.

Whether the guided math structure is new and unfamiliar or you've been at it for decades, this book will provide insight into how to improve each of the four main components of guided math: the math warm-up, the math mini-lesson, small groups and workstations, and the lesson reflection. Each of these components anchors learning with a specific focus and desired outcome. Chapter 1 will cover these four components in greater detail, explaining how and why they're effective tools for approaching your math block in a new way.

But merely having a functioning guided math classroom is not the end goal here—that's just a springboard for making your guided math block AMPED. As we approach each guided math component, we will also enhance it with a natural progression of excellent teaching and learning techniques. Chapters 2 through 6 are devoted to the steps needed to amplify your guided math block with easy-to-implement, foolproof techniques for making math class engaging and even entertaining!

Chapter 2 examines the first step toward creating an AMPED math block: careful, individualized observation of the math block that helps to give an educator heightened **attention** to planning a truly outstanding guided math experience. This heightened attention will allow educators to develop a coherent action plan for moving forward and creating a classroom culture that reflects the goals of guided math.

Chapter 3 discusses the second step: **management** of the math block in order to create a consistent, meaningful framework and flow for activities, expectations, and learning—particularly with regard to AMPED practices that inform mini-lessons and the design of workstations.

Chapter 4 tackles the third step for AMPED math blocks: best practices with regard to pedagogy and modelling math within the guided math block and how to set the right **purpose**—and pace—for each component.

Chapter 5 addresses the fourth step of the AMPED math block: the tremendous importance of leveraging **empathy**. This chapter will look at a variety of topics, from purposeful listening that gives students space and time to explain their mathematical process, to dealing with mistakes and offering effective feedback and authentic praise.

Chapter 6 looks at the fifth and final step of the AMPED math block: fully and holistically **developing** students, and their math habits, over the course of the year. This chapter discusses the importance of cultivating leadership and igniting independence in students.

The book ends with a conclusion that looks back at guided math in light of the outcomes it yields in terms of student performance.

In the end, I believe that an effective guided math block is an AMPED math block and that taking the steps that this book outlines can help transform guided math blocks. It's my hope that, in partaking of these insights, you will emerge feeling empowered and ready to tackle the challenge of redesigning or tweaking your math block into what it should be: an exciting and engaging encounter that helps your students become genuine mathematicians.

CHAPTER 1

THE GUIDED MATH STRUCTURE

As discussed earlier, guided math is not defined by following a curriculum; instead, guided math is the framework we put into place that allows us to meet with students for targeted instruction. The four components of guided math are simply the makeup of how to run the math block, and each of these components—the math warm-up, the math mini-lesson, teacher-led small groups with concurrent workstations, and the lesson reflection—is an essential piece of the guided math block puzzle. Taken together, these integral pieces create a well-rounded mathematician. Although this isn't just another book about the guided math structure, it is vital that we first discuss these four components in depth so that we can address common patterns and pitfalls, as well as the incredible potential of guided math.

For this reason, we will go through these four components, and I will share necessary information on the structure and focus for each. This overview of the components serves to align our understanding of the guided math structure. Once we establish a solid foundation for what the guided math components are, and what they work toward, we will discuss how to amp up those structures with the best practices that form the next—and most substantial—portion of the book.

THE MATH WARM-UP

We begin the guided math block with the math warm-up. The math warm-up is a short spiral-review math activity used as a way to keep past or learned concepts fresh. Because our students must absorb a constant and large amount of new math information during their short nine months in our classrooms, we know that students cannot keep all of the new learning at the forefront of their minds. As students continually add additional, rigorous information weekly, older information will naturally become "soft" or "fuzzy" as it is covered over with each new skill or concept. The math warm-up is a powerful way to begin the math learning, yet once students are trained in the process, it can be done in just five to ten minutes.

Because of the amount of new information and the pace teachers must keep to in order to adhere to the current standards framework, the math warm-up allows us a time to remind students about past concepts and skills and then have students practice and apply those concepts daily. This is an integral part of the guided math structure because it allows students to solidify information while gaining automaticity and confidence in the practice and application of older concepts. Math warm-up is also a great time to connect earlier understandings to the new learning with increasing skill as students mathematically mature through the school year.

The procedure we want to use in a math warm-up is to study the strategies and process of finding solutions, rather than just knowing an answer. When we choose a skill or problem to review as a math warm-up, our focus is on how a mathematician processes a problem.

Our focus is not simply on devising the answer to a math problem. Instead, finding the correct answer is valuable because it reinforces that our strategies and steps in problem-solving, or process, were accurate. In a math warm-up, students communicate their math understanding through sharing how their mathematical thinking led them to a strategy for solving the problem. We want students to think deeply about something, reason it out loud, and listen to others doing the same. This process intrinsically builds adaptive reasoning in our students.

Whether we find ourselves in a kindergarten classroom or an AP calculus classroom, the math warm-up is a meeting of the math minds. Students are presented with a problem. This problem should be something they have been exposed to but are not currently working on in the main learning objective for that day. It serves as a review to deepen and solidify understanding. Once you've presented students with the problem, leave time for students to work either mentally or by using a journal, turning and talking to a partner, or making a quick sketch on a personal whiteboard or scratch paper. Then, prompt students to give a signal when they have chosen a strategy and worked through the steps of problem-solving. Once most students have arrived at a strategy, invite students to share their thinking.

Academic language should be expected and used for naming problem types, strategies, methods, and steps. This approach should begin in kindergarten because it allows students to embrace the language of math while empowering them to think of themselves as mathematicians. All methods and answers should be treated with respect, as students are likely to share different strategies for solving the same problem with personal reasoning.

THE MATH MINI-LESSON

The second component in the guided math structure is the math mini-lesson, which refers to the point in the math block where the teacher shares new learning to the entire class at the same time. Based on curricular scope and sequence or district guidelines, teachers teach the priority standards, or new learning objectives, to their class in a whole-group setting. Because it is done in the whole-group setting and relates closely to the traditional teaching model, most teachers are familiar and competent with the idea of teaching a mini-lesson. In the context of guided math, the difference is in our purpose for and the time spent on this component.

Knowing that classrooms today have students working years above and below grade level, we want to do as much as possible to engage all learners during a whole-group mini-lesson by keeping lesson content on a level playing field. In a traditional whole-group lesson, students tend to be more passive observers and listeners. In guided math, by contrast, we want to focus on introducing new content while provoking all levels of learners to reason and conceptualize together. When I approach content for a mini-lesson, I begin by asking myself, "How can I present this new skill or concept in a way that builds a strong foundation of understanding while pulling in all learners?"

This broad and inclusive approach sounds unrealistic, but let's break it down so that it's easier to realize. Cognitive structure can be a valuable way to frame mini-lessons. Cognitive structure is the schema and mental models that our students have already developed as a result of exposure to previous experiences and learning—essentially, everything we have done up to this point in time. We want to access information that students have a firm understanding of so that we can help students bridge the known and the unknown. This way, they can take in the new information and run with it.

There are three categories of mini-lessons: conceptual, strategy-based, and procedural. Each provides an important purpose to our teaching that will give a clear focus to our delivery. At the same time, each serves to impart important types of math understanding for our students. This purposeful focus takes a regular lesson and creates a dynamic and shorter mini-lesson.

I'll say a bit more about how to run a fully AMPED mini-lesson in chapter 4. For now, though, the primary consideration is that not every student will be able to understand a mini-lesson's new information in one sitting of the whole group. For some, it will take many exposures and formats to reinforce new math concepts. Again, though, this is where guided math is an asset, as learning will be strengthened immediately in the small-group setting, our next component. In the mini-lesson, it is vital to mentally note those who may need reinforcement while still staying on track with pacing for the rest of the students. Teachers often struggle with stopping mini-lessons to address the needs of individual students, but this approach simply is not time effective, and it saps the attention of other students. Time is better spent following up during small groups with students who were clearly out of their depth in the mini-lesson. This approach offers close proximity in a more focused setting.

TEACHER-LED SMALL GROUPS AND WORKSTATIONS

This pair of simultaneous components is what really distinguishes a guided math block from a traditional math block—and for a good reason! In fact, I find this part of the math block the most invigorating because it is where the most impact happens for students! Teacher-led small groups and workstations are where we implement a dynamic shift in how teachers and students work and move within the room because this component is asymmetrical: at the same time that some students meet with the teacher in small groups, the rest of the students work through learning activities in groups, as partners, or independently.

In a teacher-led small group, the teacher provides the means for students to explore math concepts in a risk-free learning environment, all while targeting their specific instructional needs. The teacher is in close proximity as students work through targeted math concepts. Teachers cultivate differentiated learning as they monitor and adapt to what students need developmentally. These are not long, drawn-out lessons but should preferably involve anywhere from ten to twenty minutes of intensive time with groups of students. Because students are grouped by ability level or by needs around a particular skill, our instruction is hyper-focused, and we can accomplish a great deal in a shorter amount of time.

Concrete, pictorial, and abstract understanding are important considerations in determining how to best cover the learning objective. All three types of learning categories can be present in small-group lessons based on each group's needs. In a teacher-led small group, the teacher can address the learning objective specifically for the students present by considering their developmental levels of math understanding.

These math moments are crucial for *all levels of learners*, and this is worth repeating. In my own experience and with other teachers, the tendency is to target students who are struggling, but all students need, and benefit from, this systematic instruction. As a result, it's best to structure this component in such a way that you are able to see all students systematically and consistently.

WORKSTATIONS

Students not involved in a teacher-led small-group lesson should move throughout the room between various workstations. At each station, students work through a set number of activities, either in a self-paced structure or in a rotation system with a set time frame. Vary activities so that some can be done independently, some as partners, and some in groups.

There are many different systems, arrangements, groupings, and choices for how to run this part of the day. Factors that play into this are the ages of students, their ability levels, your classroom's resources, physical space, and the list goes on. Using the AMPED process outlined in this book will help you choose the best system for maximizing your learning outcomes in light of those factors.

The purpose of math workstations is for students to practice and apply known and newly learned skills and concepts through many formats and modalities. The new learning happens in the math mini-lesson and teacher-led small-group time. Therefore, the workstations allow students to practice and apply what they have already been exposed to. They deepen understanding, practice strategies, gain confidence and automaticity, and increase their cognitive structure. Independent workstations are not where we put new learning; instead, they generally offer a spiraled review of learned skills from the entire class term as we fold in freshly learned concepts from week to week. By filling our workstations with a spiral review of math skills, activities, and games, we cement past learning in the same way the math warm-up does.

I feel it necessary to mention that I do have one workstation, which I call an "Application Station," that focuses on newer learning. Although focused on the latest knowledge from the small-group instruction, my Application Station runs a few days behind the small-group lesson. I want students to have an understanding and a mastery of the basics before I send them over to work independently. In this way, the Application Station experience helps provide the best chance for my students to have success while providing a record of learning from which I can take a grade consistently.

As we approach guided math, we have to let go of the "matching" stations. It is instructionally sound to have students working on many different skills within a math block. The purpose of math workstations is to allow students to apply and strengthen what they understand mathematically. To work independently at workstations, students must be familiar with the math topics being addressed. This desire to match our stations to our new learning objective (so that the entire room is doing place value, for instance) stems, I think, from the pressure of having our learning objectives displayed for a pop-in evaluation. If someone walks into our classroom and sees that our new learning objective is measurement, we might feel a sense of pressure that every student should be working on that skill, no matter where they are in their workstations. This effectiveness of this approach to learning new material, however, is simply not grounded in research.

Our purpose in workstations is to deepen content understanding, build fluency and automaticity, and ultimately create a well-rounded math experience for students. As students become proficient in new skills, procedures, and concepts that are taught in mini-lessons and teacher-led small groups, I begin to fold those new skills into stations so students can practice them in all the formats and modalities. Even then, I still want a variety of skills being represented in workstations at all times.

THE LESSON REFLECTION

As our final component in the guided math block, we close out learning with a reflection. This lesson closure can look and feel different from day to day, and variety is key! Regardless of format, though, our focus is on providing ways for students to reflect, grow, and change for the better. After all, each day is an opportunity to refine and improve.

We begin lesson reflection with a whole-group reflection that provides opportunities for students to consider the thinking, learning, and work they have done within the math block. We can take this time to praise connections, procedures, understandings, behaviors, and even increased knowledge—the list goes on! We reflect on the learning and the math block in any capacity.

There are several formats for framing lesson reflections. An object reflection provides a question that stems from a concrete object. For example, the teacher might hold up a puzzle piece and say, "What is still puzzling to you?" Object reflection can also be accomplished through pictures, graphics, and popular topics. The more creative the question stem, the more students will want to respond. Seasonal fun, sports teams, and current events make terrific spin-offs for reflection questions at any age. For example, during the playoffs for basketball, we can show an action shot from a recent game and ask, "How did you set up, carry through, and score today in math?" or "What procedure did you do that was worth three points?" We can also perform lesson reflection through a variety of other activities, such as exit tickets, question and response, reviewing keywords, or by attaching a personal connection to the math lesson. At other times, an assessment is simply how we need to close out.

The lesson reflection is usually the first component to be cut, but if done purposefully, it is one of the most potent ways to keep students accountable for their roles in the learning. The more you reflect on the different points of understanding within the math block, the better the reflection gets. Students need instruction and refinement with reflecting, so try to keep at it and challenge yourself to make reflection different each day of the week. Inspired prompts and questions result in enthusiastic and meaningful responses! How can you reach the unique students sitting in your room?

AMPED

With an understanding of the four components that create the framework of a guided math block, we can now take a closer look at the moments within these components to amplify our instruction. Simply having the guided math structure in place does not yield the full potential of an amplified math block. In this section, we'll reflect on how to address the moments that magnify and electrify our outcomes for the better.

CHAPTER 2

ATTENTION:
RE-ENVISIONING
GUIDED MATH

Have you ever stepped into a classroom that is not your own and as you glanced around and took in the sights and sounds, you began to sense what day-to-day life and learning in that space felt like? Close your eyes and recall the rooms that had a strong academic "feel" with caring undertones. The environment pulls you in as you feel yourself brighten with curiosity, joy, and a willingness to learn. Immediately, I think of a strong connection to the teacher, a sense of belonging within the environment, and positive academic memories—moments of growth or success regardless of subject area. Think for a moment about a specific classroom that you know to be highly effective. Slowly scan the room; consider the learning structures in place, the teacher's position and demeanor, and the physical space. What do you notice? Pay close attention. Then, do the same exercise for the less sufficient classroom you've set foot into—the classrooms that had palpable tension, confusion, lack of engagement, or disorganization. Inside the four walls of our classrooms lives a learning environment that we, as teachers, are responsible for!

The first step in creating an AMPED math block is paying closer attention to what is currently happening during our math block minutes. We can begin this deep dive into our math blocks *as they are* by paying close attention to the reoccurring routines, practices, and expectations happening in our classroom.

As classroom teachers, observation is often something we do on autopilot. We can tell you what Shane will do before he even has the idea to do it. We study our students and learn their idiosyncrasies intently. Although we carefully observe student behaviors regularly, we also need to cultivate a different type of attention to our instruction, pedagogical roles, and actions. This attention requires truly being real and "in the moment" through an unbiased lens. It's hard to get an impartial observation when you have designed the entire room, structure, and ongoing instruction, so think of pulling away from your identity within your classroom's walls and looking in as an outsider.

The best observation would be that of a stranger with absolutely no bias sitting unobtrusively as we conduct our entire math block. Such a stranger would hold no preconceived ideas about your instruction or the abilities of your students in the room. This stranger would know and recognize the markers of guided math instruction, evidence of learning, effective strategies, and the importance of collaborative learning. Because this outside observation isn't very easy to come by, though, sometimes the next best thing is the camera.

If you can set up a camera in a way that will capture and record all of the goings-on of your math block, then you have an unbiased tool that will give you a picture of not only your role but also of the role each student takes part in throughout your math block. Remember, though, we are looking for impartial observation. Don't do your dog and pony show. Don't draw attention to the camera. Think about your run-of-the-mill, it's-Thursday-again math lesson. No one is going to see this magnificent mayhem except you, so keep it real.

Your potential for growth from attention depends on the depth you are willing to go to change what you know isn't on target. Our focus is on amplifying the entire experience: ourselves as the teacher, our behavior expectations, our student learning opportunities, and, ultimately, our student outcomes.

If you are sitting poolside enjoying summer vacation as you read this book, then we will have to rely on our vivid math block moments of past years as we go through this exercise of attention. I challenge you to pull up the memories of the lessons where you had to brush yourself off and cue the positive self-talk to continue to push forward. For me, these are the types of moments when I plan and prepare a lesson but a non-related behavior issue interferes and my motivation goes by the wayside. Lessons where students have so many questions that I have to look at my delivery and possibly admit that it's me not them. Other times, it is my lack of time spent planning that results in lessons that I know could be better or more engaging, but I just didn't have the motivation on the front end. In the moment, I find myself disappointed because I know what needed to happen for students.

One time in particular I had prepared a strategy-based lesson for my young primary class in the first weeks of school where we were going to use props in a ten frame. I had found some superhero bean bags we would use to fill the life-size ten frame at the carpet area. I was being observed by a new administrator, which added a layer of anticipation and excitement about the lesson. As I began, student engagement was palpable. Students were seated around the large carpet-sized ten frame and perfectly postured to receive a chance to build a number with the superhero bean bags. I stated a number and handed a student a bean bag. He excitedly squeezed the bean bag, revealing that they lit up and made noise. A *tiny* detail I had not checked before designing this lesson experience. The entire class erupted in screams, laughter, and shouts of joy. I never fully got those students back to the right instructional level, yet I plowed on through with my dog and pony show, which was more of a *Jurassic Park* movie experience than anything resembling a math lesson. I only met eyes with the administrator once during the mini-lesson, and she quickly looked away. Two decades of teaching and I am still not over it. Those moments do not define us as math teachers. But they do ground us and push us to grow. Attention is not judgement. It is introspection and growth potential.

Allowing attention to our lessons from planning to lesson reflection can be a vulnerable place to start. Do you feel your shoulders tense? But I have severe behaviors! There's not enough time to be as effective as I need to be. There's too much to cover, and I have too many students who struggle! These are all valid and real issues in today's classrooms. The AMPED guided math block will help us address all of these relevant roadblocks. Let's go beyond the hardships and truly study what is happening. Then, we can make the best plan to handle these tough issues.

As we watch our math block unfold, we want to pay close attention to these three questions:

- What is present?
- What is being reinforced?
- What is surprising?

Each of these questions will reveal valuable information we can use to amplify our math block. If you are struggling to answer one or more of these questions, you may need to observe more than one of your math blocks in order to begin to see patterns.

Let's talk through a brief exercise that can help us schematize what we've observed.

THE WAY THINGS ARE

Reflect on what drew your attention during your self-observation. What is already present? What is already happening in our classrooms? When we answer these questions, we want to take notice of the markers of guided math. Are all four components present: the math warm-up, math mini-lesson, small group and workstations, and reflection? Perhaps you have been doing a component but notice that the focus is not entirely on target. Maybe the small group is only a reteaching station and not really differentiated learning for all students systematically.

Take note of the pacing that is present. Are you conducting a schedule that allows all students to thrive? Do you have too many fast finishers? Is there a breakdown in engagement during workstations? What do you notice that you love? What part of the math block renders the most engagement? Why? Create a list of what is presently working within those components and why you think that is the case. If there is a negative issue present (such as lack of engagement, unfinished work, fast finishers, lack of quality in work, etc.), write it down. As we continue through and things pop into your head, add them to the list.

What is being reinforced? As you observe and reflect more on your teaching day to day, you will likely notice certain behavior patterns emerge. If your reaction to these patterns is not positive, then consider how these behaviors began and how they are being reinforced. In all likelihood, the root of problematic behavior can be addressed and changed. If things are going well, take note of how those positive moments are reinforced in order to apply those practices to other areas.

The final question we want to address is, "What surprises you as you observe and reflect?" Perhaps something that you didn't realize was happening, or a byproduct of something within the math block, draws your attention. This can provide insight into student roles, teaching practices, and outcomes—all of which we will dig into as we transform our math block.

This observation and reflection list will bring clarity and focus to the current structure. It will reveal the areas where you are strong and the areas that have room to be amplified. As you work through the five steps to an AMPED math block, this will be your working list. We may also reveal new levels of attention that require additional consideration. This is a working list. Let's keep an open mind and a keen eye to what we can reveal through these next steps.

THE WAY THINGS ARE NOT

As teachers, we know that what is missing from our classrooms is just as valid as what is present. In that light, we want to take notice of what we yearn for our math block to be. By that same token, then, we also need to note the distinctly missing moments—such as lesson closure or reflection time, or not seeing enough students in a small group because of the current way our block is structured. What can we notice that is *not* in place the way we would like it to be? Do workstations end up being worksheets? Are students stuck without support? Is there anything that is missing from your dream math block? What would you like to have in place if you could?

Review your self-observation again, paying attention to "what is not" in all aspects and add to your list these areas that you wish to implement. If any items in your two lists—"What Is" and "What Is Not"—seem to be overlapping, give a star to them. Those two items may both end up on the list, but they potentially address the same issue.

DEVISING AN ACTION PLAN

Now that we have lists of what is presently problematic and conspicuously missing from our math block, we need to create our action plan! An action plan is a proposed course of action for reaching a goal. An action plan allows us to focus intently on the steps to take to create the most impact. For each teacher, this will have a different look, and if you work through this book more than once, your action plan will likely change for you each time. When creating your action plan, you want to stop and notice the items on the lists that are pulling the most strongly for you—not what you think *others* want to see from you or what looks best, but what would indeed create the best learning environment for you and your students to flourish daily.

As you brainstorm for your action plan, I feel it necessary to note that comparison is the thief of joy. Perhaps the teacher next door has been praised for flexible seating options during workstations, but the idea of having that type of movement and chaos going on in your room breaks you out in hives. If that's the case, then "flexible seating" should not be on your list. Period. The items on your lists are unique to the incredible teacher *that you are*. Stop worrying about the fantastic teacher next door, and remind yourself that you are just as amazing! Instead, think about the changes that would be impactful for you and *all* your students.

Sadly, I have seen incredibly smart and capable teachers run a math block in a defeated and frustrated mindset because of the pattern of hyper-focusing on one student and their challenging behavior. I'm hanging my head in shame just thinking about how I have done the same. I challenge you to notice this, stop it immediately, and give the 99 percent your full and beautiful abilities as their teacher.

To further home in on a plan, focus on components, teaching practices, and items within your control. The items you are considering for your action plan should address the entire math block and should not be tied to individual student behavior. Be careful to keep your action plan targeted on structure, instruction, roles, and procedures and not about the meltdown Mason had today and will likely have again tomorrow. When you are a positive and radiant force focusing on greatness, the result will be greatness. What you focus on will continue to be the center of the learning. It's not easy to establish this new pattern, but I challenge you to practice this for the students that show up ready and willing to learn from you.

With your brainstorming done, it's time to pull together a focused action plan. Going back through your list of areas to address, make a box around no more than three items that you know would create the best math block. These will be your primary focus for this school year, term, or semester. Underline things that are less intensive to change, such as eliminating an ineffective workstation or creating a better room arrangement for the flow of the components. These are things you can change without too much consideration or time factored in.

If you have come to this point in the process and have not had a moment of realization, consider asking to observe other teachers during their math block. It can be just as useful to watch teachers in other grade levels, too. Allow yourself to appreciate and understand different ways of running a math block using the guided math structure. Recognize when things are present and when they are missing, and how that affects the overall effectiveness of learning.

Attention amplifies our math block because it keeps us keenly aware of the environment we are creating for our students and how they are functioning within that environment. Teaching is dynamic and always evolving, so attention is the first step in running the amplified math block. When there is a breakdown, we notice and create an action plan to address it.

Review your focus and create a new action plan list with your three main items. Underneath each item leave some space to write in what needs to happen in order for this to become an integral part of your math block. Do you need to reconsider the current timing and structure to incorporate these changes? Perhaps you need to pursue resources or materials for a new endeavor. If it is more of a behavioral adjustment within a structure, we will be addressing those needs in the coming steps! Formulate or record the necessary steps to reach the goal of implementation. Some may be obvious, and some will be revealed as we continue through this process.

READY FOR LAUNCH

To begin this next section, I want to revisit that experience of a time you walked into a classroom where the engagement was as sky-high as the learning. Let's lean into this experience and consider how such a classroom culture was established. Typically, these AMPED classroom environments are this way year after year. The teacher creates an AMPED culture regardless of the challenges of the class roster each term. Remember, though, that the learning environments we produce do not happen by chance. They do not depend on the students or teachers in the room; instead, they result from a higher set of expectations and procedures that transcend the day-to-day content or social situations.

One of my favorite times of the year is classroom setup. The potential for greatness is pulsating through my veins, and I am insanely inspired to create a new learning environment. My motivation has highs and lows as I tackle all of the moving parts and pieces of this time of the school year, but overall, it's a thrilling time of hope and preparation.

During classroom setup, I walk the halls to visit teachers around me. Some teachers are truly gifted in creating an environment for learning. I walk in and just absorb their process. I notice the organization, the setup, the learning spaces, and the considerations that went into each decision. As great as we may be at our teaching craft, we can still constantly keep that fire blazing by learning from those around us who are also honing their craft on their journey.

Once we have established how we plan to run the components of our guided math block, the next step is to introduce and practice this structure during a time frame that I call "launch." Typically, this launch phase is only two to four weeks long. Older students can launch into the full guided math workshop more quickly, and younger students will need more time, explanation, and practice to get there. This practice is the avenue to creating the exact, minute-by-minute math block; it establishes a routine and structure that we'll need for the entire year. There is a formula for how we practice during the launch phase. During launch, we are teaching regular content, followed by the critical learning of a new procedure. This pattern continues until we have all of the expectations in place for establishing a sense of "business as usual" in our guided math block.

Launch begins with a surface-level introduction of the components and overall flow of the general math block. Next, we work our way through every student role and expectation, whether in whole-group, small-group, or collaborative structures. Finally, we introduce content for each component. This tiered practice is a vital part of creating desired behavior and learning opportunities for the year.

Regardless of age group or grade level, carry out the launch phase in a strict—even rigid—format of delivery. Expectations should be higher than anything students have experienced. The way to get there is to teach the expectation, then model the correct procedure or response, then immediately practice those ideals multiple times. No matter the response you get, demand better. Show the response again. Push energy and enthusiasm into the moment and practice again. Continue this repetition until you have an even better response to your expectations than you believed you could get. Then do it again. Do this daily for the entire launch period, and every time things get too comfortable thereafter. This routine establishes a high level of engagement and expectations as the norm.

While launch is rigid in terms of expectations, this does not mean that the tone during the launch phase is harsh or demanding. In fact, it's the perfect time to cultivate the buy-in we desire from our students. This is done through honest give and take. We practice, we discuss, we practice again. Our tone is confident in the structure and plan we are implementing, caring in getting students to the highest level of readiness, and cautious in disallowing any action that undermines the plan or learning potential. Students see my thrill of positive outcomes and my disappointment in missing the targeted expectation through a real and honest relationship.

Correct responses and procedures open the door to new learning opportunities while the opposite results in a loss of privilege. There is a direct correlation between desired behavior and rewarding learning experiences. Whether students are five years old or fifteen years old, they must perform to expectations in order to unlock new levels of learning in the classroom. As easily as they can unlock these levels, they can also lose them. It has to be a fluid give and take for the students to learn that they have a real responsibility to the structure of the math block. The launch phase is not done in an ugly tone or a dictatorial mentality but rather through consistent explanation, the immediate practice of the expectation, and detailed feedback. It is important that although launch is the strictest time of the year, there are supportive undertones.

Whether you are introducing how the students move within the classroom or how to complete a station activity, follow the same practice procedure: teach the explicit expectation, model, practice, provide feedback, and repeat. Remember the list of items from your observation that you want to correct? The launch phase is when we can create new and ongoing habits to eliminate undesired results and amplify our classroom environment. Pay close attention to those specific areas you noticed and wanted to correct.

During the launch phase, it's likely that stamina will break at some point. When that happens and I notice a decline in the productive hum of the practice activity, I will give the signal to initiate our cleanup procedure. We then come back to the whole group to discuss. This is an open forum discussion, but I am also carefully leading us to self-discovery and areas of concern that need to be addressed. We may go back out and try a second time or wrap things up with some independent work in order to stay on track with our learning in the remaining time frame.

This is how I work through the launch phase. We learn about a new math experience, create norms and procedures, test them out, then come back and fine-tune those norms until we create the best fit for every learner. It's a healthy give and take, but I am most definitely steering the ship. We practice the same new workstation and fine-tune it for a few days before moving on to the next. Every class and every grade level will pace through this launch process differently. I hesitate to say a hard number of times to practice something or to remain on the same workstation because it will depend on how students are functioning and their stamina for the activity. It is important to uphold power in the process. Every positive action and expectation that is met brings us closer to unlocking a new math-learning experience.

It may take longer to get comfortable with a particular activity, and yesterday may have gone wonderfully while today is falling apart. It's all a part of the launch phase. When I first started out, it was so hard for me to accept that a class can enjoy a two-week span of excellence and then bottom out completely out of the blue. Do I run outside to check the status of the full moon? Sometimes. But it's just part of life. Don't let it defeat all of the excellence you have poured into your math block. Address issues and move forward.

BUILDING UPON YOUR FOUNDATION

Creating the ideal environment for learning only happens over time, through small moments that we explicitly put into place. Beyond the attentional, intentional, practice-driven changes that I've outlined above, there are five building blocks to a high-yield classroom, which frankly aren't going to bend your brain or shock you but are integral for capitalizing on that ideal learning environment once they've been established. Until we get the right climate and culture in place, these building blocks don't produce the mathematical returns on our instructional investment. This is why I feel it's important to emphasize that these steps come only *after* we have the correct driving forces in place.

The first building block is to enhance content knowledge. Every student in the room can make learning leaps with the right scaffolding or challenges in instruction. While we can't control the actual standards we are required to teach within our grade level, we can control our delivery of the content. How much information do we need to chunk to each student, and should our approach be more structured, ensuring small successful steps to build confidence? Or perhaps a more open-ended challenge approach to stimulate a high-flying student or group ready to explore a new math skill with soaring confidence?

The second building block to a high-yield classroom is optimizing math minutes. This involves infusing math into the natural flow of our structure. Every minute is important and maximized. When students enter the room, the warm-up is already in place. Routines are in motion and expectations are unwavering so the content is king. While transitioning from one guided math component to the next, students are already visualizing and anticipating their next math experience. With a firm routine set, teacher pacing is in tune with student performance and productivity. When the productive hum begins to falter, the teacher makes precise pacing decisions that enhance the math experience. Tightened pacing can truly eliminate unwanted behaviors, but be careful to always pace to the natural stamina of the class—that 85 percent makeup of the room. We will always have the fast and furious and the sweet and slow represented, but they are not the norm for pacing.

Third, we can leverage our learning environments by providing ways to encourage mathematical practices. Mathematical practice standards are present when we create math explorations and math tasks for students to actively engage in. Typically, I notice these standards being met most frequently in a math warm-up and during student workstations or rotations. During these times, students actively take part in the learning rather than sitting passively in an instructional lesson. Mathematical practice standards that actively engage students in math explorations turn principles of math instruction into real-life math applications on a daily basis.

The fourth and fifth building blocks of a high-yield classroom work together. These blocks speak to the frameworks I discussed as necessary for creating an inclusive math mini-lesson. We want to build on existing knowledge and develop a deeper understanding. These two building blocks go back to the foundation of how students develop mathematically. Before taking on a new skill or concept, consider the students' current cognitive structures: the skills and concepts, mental models, and schema the students will draw upon to create meaning. Next, consider how to bridge to the new learning so that students must make connections from their old knowledge to the new knowledge. Students are constantly constructing and reconstructing their understanding, and one of the challenges we have as teachers is to facilitate this rather than doing it for them. In effect, we provide the tools, the initial task, the questions, and the opportunity for exploration and discovery rather than methods and procedures.

BUILDING RELATIONSHIPS

At the beginning of my career, I took an authoritarian approach to relationships in the classroom. Somewhere along the way, I internalized the old adage that circulates about teaching: "Don't smile until Christmas." This implies teachers should begin their year as strict, uninviting individuals who maintain tight control over their students by restricting their personal, relational interactions. Thankfully, though, it didn't take long to realize that I was creating an oppositional environment that was more about maintaining order than authentic relationships or learning. To be sure, there's great value in maintaining order and high expectations in our classrooms, but we can also do so with a smile. When we smile at our students, we reassure their nerves, we let them know that our classroom is a caring place to be, and we send the message that learning is fun.

It's important to be accepting of all students. We need to empathize with our students in order to understand how to teach them best. If I am struggling to connect with an individual, I sit in their spot and try to consider their thoughts and feelings in relation to the classroom and to myself as their teacher. Then, I begin the conversations and connections with the student that will convey that I desire to be a positive part of their life.

We can be caring, warm, and nurturing but not in a permissive way that tells students they can act out without consequences. To do this, we need to focus on the potential best in each student. We need to place an emphasis on creating order and structure in order to have the highest quality work and high expectations for learning. We need to be mentally present for students, showing them that we accept who they are, right here, today, while expecting them to grow and become their best potential self through the school year together.

We need to provide guidance and structure in how students interact with us and with each other through all components of the math block. We can do this by practicing learning and listening intently, as we'll discuss in more depth in chapter 5. High-performing students need to know they are cared for, but they also need to be pressed to excel to their greatest potential. We need to have confidence in students' ability to learn information and create meaning and understanding with the new skills and concepts.

Having genuine confidence in our students shapes their thoughts and actions into believing they are capable mathematicians. The amplified math block consists of a classroom full of empowered mathematicians who are ready to take on new information through healthy collaborations and high-quality work.

CHAPTER 3

MANAGEMENT:
KEEPING LEARNING
ELECTRIFYING

Management is the cornerstone of a well-executed, truly AMPED math block. With a vision and plan of action in place for overhauling your math block, you'll still need to adopt processes that engineer—and re-engineer—success. In guided math, the level of management is most evident in the small group and workstation time. In these components, students both young and old thrive with a consistent set of expectations in place. When students understand that there is a consistent flow to the math block with consistent expectations, they can more easily understand their role within those guidelines. Also, when you introduce new content to your math block, students can give it their full attention because the format of how the class time will run is consistent. We manage the classroom to create a frame of expectations. The breathtaking insights inside that frame are created daily by well-managed students.

In guided math, there are two central systems for managing workstations. The first is a system whereby students self-pace through a series of activities that the teacher has put out for completion in a certain amount of time, such as over one week. This system works well with students who need differentiation while out at workstations and who may have different expectations for how to pace themselves based on their ability levels. Students have a way of marking where they have been and what they did there, and they ultimately self-manage their workflow. A math menu, a clip chart, and an interactive digital board are three examples of how students may show accountability within a self-pacing system. When using this type of system, I match the ability level of the students to the math menu. Younger students color a shape on a math menu that matches a shape on a math center box to show they have completed it. For older students, I allow them to check off an activity and write a short reflection of what they did. The self-pacing system can be used with success in any grade level, but there are some factors to consider.

With a self-pacing management system, students need a way of staying accountable for work, and they need a way to receive feedback that lets them know if they are on pace to finish the required work choices in the allotted time frame. If your students generally struggle with choosing appropriate tasks, pacing, or remembering to mark and track their progress, this system may not be the perfect fit.

The second central system for managing guided math workstations is the rotation system. This system is a more structured approach to running workstations that explicitly designates where students go, what they do there, and for how long. The teacher can certainly add choices to the rotations, but generally speaking, this system supports students who need more structure to thrive. It can also help teachers who need more structure to manage behaviors.

In a rotation system, students have a carousel of activities they will rotate through in a given time frame. A full rotation can take place within a class period, two to four days, or a full week. There are many options for the number of stations, length of time spent at each, and what students are doing within a station, but the structure remains consistent. Students visit a certain number of workstations over a set amount of time, and that does not change; only the activities within those stations will change.

Consistency is imperative, and we want to uphold that in every class period. When students understand this routine, our job becomes much more about providing quality learning experiences and less about managing unwanted behaviors. Step one is choosing the management system that works well for you and your students and that helps you all reach the fullest potential. Step two is upholding the system daily. How will that look for you?

Through the years, station rotations have taken on many shapes and forms for me. I have used a math menu, a clip system, a digital display, a wall chart, and the list goes on. Each had its way of tracking and managing our daily work, and each served its purpose. It's not about one system over another, but more about experimenting with what will work for you. I have had years where I jumped from one system to another due to the behaviors that were present.

As I first embraced this new way of conducting my math block, I first experimented with the self-pacing system. I had decided to implement a math menu with first graders. On a sheet of paper, I created a simple table of ten boxes with a shape image in each box. Then I purchased ten clear bins with lids. Each bin got a shape die-cut on the front that corresponded with a shape on the math menu I had created for students. The math menu paper was stapled to each child's math folder. I explained that students had ten stations to visit over two weeks' time. I also did this in a digital format with fourth graders the same year in collaboration with another teacher.

To keep track of what they had done, they would color or mark the shape as they completed each math activity. Students marked their station work on their math menus with careful consideration and worked through their math menus in the allotted time without concern. I believed I had finally found the secret to running workstations and looked forward to this as my favorite part of the day. I was on a math high. Although my station activities did not vary much in format, the students didn't seem to mind, and I received praise and accolades from visitors who witnessed this part of our day. It was a pinnacle year for me.

The very next year, I changed schools within the district and began math in the very same way. My experience was what guided math nightmares are made of. The noise level was deafening, dice and counters were flying through the air, arguments ensued, and I honestly don't know if there was a math menu in sight. I remember feeling like the room was spinning and I questioned why I ever became a teacher. Fear welled up inside my stomach as I wondered if I possessed the ability to manage students at all.

With a hot head and a pounding heart, I shouted to stop and shut the entire thing down. That is *not* how I run my classroom. As I looked around, much to my dismay, I realized that I was the only one in charge, and therefore, this mess had to be fixed by *me*. I didn't know where to start, and I was so devastated that my favorite part of the day was no longer a viable option and had little hope of returning.

I learned an incredible amount in that pivotal year. As much as I loved the self-pacing system, my students did not possess the management skills or maturity to self-pace and self-manage. The only way we would survive was to try a more structured approach. I was gutted at the idea of changing something that had been such a positive experience for me. I questioned every choice that led me up to this point. I compared, cried, critically assessed, and came to the conclusion that the structure was effective but I had work to do on management and math tasks.

MANAGING LEARNING GROUPS

I'm not alone in my struggles to keep workstations consistent, focused, and generative. When I work with teachers regarding the implementation of guided math, one of the most frequent topics brought up is grouping students to work together. It is such a hot topic because dysfunctional student learning groups can be a road-block on the highway to implementation. Thankfully, there are many ways to troubleshoot workstations, or other small-group activities, that simply don't seem to work, and there are many alternatives for managing groups toward success.

It's worth reiterating that grouping students can be done in many ways to accommodate many learning goals. For the sake of keeping things focused on amplifying learning-group outcomes, though, let's analyze how effective groups function rather than looking at how to group students by learning levels. Whether you have created mixed-ability groups, like-ability groups, partners, or flexibly changing groups, it's crucial that you focus on the functionality of the students within those varied grouping situations.

My first few years of grouping students are a bit of a blur, mostly because my anxiety was high while I tried out various structures. I didn't care much about student outcomes. It was all about if they could even do it. Will they know how to play a game or complete an activity without direct teacher instruction? I had serious doubts because of my own educational math experience, but it's wonderful now to see how comfortable students as young as kindergarteners are with this structure.

When student learning groups work well together, the class-room is buzzing with students sharing understanding with each other. Students are checking their thinking, communicating under-standing, justifying reasoning; the mathematical practice standards are living and breathing around the room. It's both heartwarming and invigorating to be a part of a functional math-learning environment in action.

When we believe students can't do something, then likely they will live up to that expectation. But believing students will do well in a group dynamic doesn't magically make it happen, either. Countless times I have toiled, creating the perfect groupings of the students in the classroom or on the placement cards, but in reality, the mixture that worked on paper did not work in the flesh. I believed these groupings were the perfect fit for my goals and my students' needs, but the reality was something, ahem . . . different.

To amplify learning groups, we need to study their dysfunctions first. From this point we can determine if an issue might hinge on academic abilities, carrying out social and group norms, or perhaps a certain one-student issue that has nothing to do with the group or partner dynamic. Until we identify the problem, we will keep barking out orders and expecting things to magically be better next time. As we both know, it won't. And over time, it will become impossible to teach in small groups with any consistent dysfunction.

As I discussed in the previous chapter, I lovingly refer to the first four weeks of implementing a math block structure as "the launch phase." Students know that during launch they learn expectations, work on understanding student and group roles, and earn all of the new and exciting privileges that our math block will enjoy in the near future. Launch is a time of constant feedback and discussion, and it requires a lot of attention. We don't want to settle into less than our best because, as time goes on, things will get comfortable and begin to slip naturally.

Because much of our students' work time is spent with peers and around the room, all of these interactions are introduced, practiced, discussed, and even tracked visually (yet very simply) for our growth during launch. Toward that end, addressing learning groups has to be organic and authentic to what is happening in the room.

During the launch phase you should be particularly attentive to group dysfunction. Try flexibly arranging partners and groups within the launch time frame to find the best fit for students' personalities. For me, the resulting group arrangements are not what I had on paper. Instead, they are the result of testing out how students work together and which skill sets work best together. I begin with academic grouping, then I layer on social grouping needs, and finally, I make modifications for the unique challenges present in the room that year. It's like a three-layered cake of learning group dynamics: academic, social, and behavioral. When learning groups function at their fullest potential, it can feel like you are on a mountaintop of momentum. It's a fantastic, yet fleeting, feeling. Although it may be wonderful for two weeks straight, we can't control the ins and outs of every personality and mood in the room for 180 days.

Student-group interactions and performance will ebb and flow. For this reason, it's important to go back to the practices outlined in the "attention" chapter; we want to have a pulse on what's happening and whether issues will pass on their own or need addressing. Like with anything, variety is the spice of life. Mixing up groupings once a week, once a month, or regularly will amplify and energize the room. You'll also want to review launch norms or, better yet, update them when changing up groups. What we need in month one of school is not the same as what we need in month three and so on. Changing up groups is a great way to keep motivations and expectations at the forefront of students' minds, validate current issues, and grow independence in the room.

MANAGING DISRUPTIONS

For students who do not meet expectations or norms, regardless of changing up the grouping and initiating both positive and negative reinforcers, the last option is to have a student work out of the group and next to the small-group area that you directly facilitate. This pro-cedure was something I created in the dark hours of the night out of desperation. I had no tricks left in my management playbook, and I was almost ready to give up learning groups. After trying every group and considering the negative cycle and impact in the room, I went to a place I try to never go: separating the child.

I wasn't able to teach in a small group with the type of behavior one particular child was displaying when in any type of grouped sit-uation. I was at a loss. The whole class was being affected, and I could not get the situation turned around. I could not foster any buy-in, no matter what I did to incentivize or penalize situations. I was out of grouping options and desperate to keep the guided math structure for everyone else in the room who deserved it.

I acquired an extra student desk and placed it in the area of my small-group teaching. I gathered the independent station work this particular student would be responsible for doing that day and I placed it at this satellite desk. When it came time to release students to workstations and pull my first small group, I sent them out but asked the one student to stay behind for a second with me. Then, I brought him over and explained that this was where his work would be completed. It was a matter-of-fact, honest conversation. I told the student that my expectations for him hadn't been met, and that this desk would be where he would complete his work. "So for today," I told him, "your goal is to work independently on your stations at this desk, and I'm here if you need anything."

Although the student was upset at this, he sat. He didn't work, but he sat. The other students began their workstations, and we were at full functionality for the first time since I could remember. It was a real turning point in taking back control and allowing the learners in the room to do what they needed to be successful. My heart beat quickly and was cautiously breaking for the separated student, but I noticed the other students were energized, relaxed, and engaged in their workstations.

Throughout the day, the student I pulled out sat through my small-group teaching multiple times with different groups and their different needs. He didn't do station work, but he listened, even answered questions beginning with the second group, and we had a time of quiet understanding. Now, it wasn't perfect. But it was so much better than the disruptions that would have been happening to the learning groups out in the room.

Pulling students out, while extreme, is an effective way to separate dysfunction from the rest of the class and address it privately. In these situations, students want to be a part of a group, but something is causing them to act out and mess that up. We have to be willing to dive in and work on the issue. So, the motivator in separating a student from workstation groups is to allow time for the student to realize how the room *should* look and feel when functioning. This realization doesn't happen instantly. It's ok if the student just sits in contemplation for a bit, refusing to work. The student has to understand they must find a way to fit into the learning environment in a positive way and not the other way around. This should not be a dramatic calling out or embarrassing punishment but rather framed as a way to pull the student in close in order to take care of the issue together. Be clear that the goal is for the student to meet expectations in order to get placed back in a group. This should all be done privately and respectfully with the out-of-compliance student.

Trying to get compliance from someone who is acting out means we have to understand the student's perspective and meet those needs—even if we have to work harder to do it. Rather than matching a student's attitude and aggression, we need to do what we can to be the antidote to it. Students need to know that *we* will make the effort because we need *them* to make the effort. It's hard. Plain and simple.

Pulling students out is actually not only a place for working with behavior issues, but also a safe place for any student having a rough day and needing close proximity to a teacher or a break from learning groups. When a student is struggling with anything, such as a death in the family or the loss of a pet, this is a way to be close but still teach and carry on with the day for the other students. Any student can be pulled out of groups as needed. Most never need it, but having a designated place in the room already available allows you to continue teaching while also handling extraordinary situations that arise for students. I would never call the desk "the pullout desk" out loud or near students. That's just for us, as educators.

Having a designated spot in the room makes it less demeaning for students when they are separated for not meeting expectations. We want to address the actual issue at hand and to do so we need students to feel accepted and a part of the group. Sending disruptive students to a "bad chair" makes that an uphill battle so the pullout desk should be framed more as a safe space in the room.

MANAGING GROUP OBJECTIVES

So, what is the overall goal of learning groups? There are three points I like to explain, model, and highlight with students regarding learning groups. The first trait I look for in a learning group is for students to discuss the concepts being learned. Students have permission to share their knowledge and thinking on the current workstation objective with a partner or a person in their group. Math warm-ups are a great way to model, for the entire class, how these collaborative, process-driven discussions can unfold.

Depending on the workstation goal, students may be defining a term together, naming a strategy to use, picking the right formula, or any range of related math thinking relevant to the skill being applied. Visuals and academic sentence starters really fast track the conversations you want for students. An academic word stem board is a great way to help students choose things to discuss. Here are some prompts to consider:

- I notice . . . so I think . . .
- The strategy that I think of is . . .
- A vocabulary word that goes with this is . . .
- The rule for this type of problem is . . .

Students know what these discussions entail because they are modeled during the math warm-up. Coming from a background of being painfully shy, a word stem board that essentially *forced* me to read a sentence starter was a huge relief. I wasn't too shy to read aloud; I was too shy to assert my own thoughts or opinions. Word stems pose the same opportunity for shy students, and second-language learners also benefit from them as well.

Our second objective is that we want students to check for understanding with at least one other person in their learning group. This check-in can come at different points during the activity depending on the nature of the station. If the station entails an interactive game that two students are playing, this check-in will happen naturally within the game. In other settings, be explicit at setting up checkpoints for students, like meeting with a buddy after two problems to make sure partners are on the right track or trading task cards to compare. Students can even be instructed to do a workstation together until they agree on their answers.

The third objective we look for in a learning group is seeing students encouraging their peers to achieve. We want to create functional groups with *working ease* to them. When discussing this, I look for ways for students to share how it made a difference that their partner told them not to give up, reminded them of a step they forgot, or gave them a positive word of encouragement when needed.

Positive interactions create positive communities. We want a nurturing and encouraging environment throughout the room.

Focusing on one objective per week is an easy way to highlight them equally. Then, for the fourth week of each month, pick a trait that your class simply needs extra help with regularly. Where does the time come from to have these learning-group meetings? Easy! Hold a simple, three-minute discussion or "locker-room chat" before you send students out to workstations for the day or as a daily wrap-up and reflection. Hopefully, the more time we put into these positive reinforcement conversations, the less time we spend disciplining and reteaching dysfunction. But these are conversations; they should feel natural and not like a formal lesson.

The procedure for managing groups through reinforcement is done like a math formula. Apply consistent steps from problem to solution. Beginning with the desired expectation, explain exactly how you want every moment to take place within the desired procedure. Reinforce those expectations every time they are practiced through feedback. If anything needs adjusting, make it clear to all students through explanation, practice, and reinforcing feedback.

Draw attention to an interaction where students exemplified a desired trait. If you are reinforcing a practiced expectation, break down how that successful interaction happened, giving praise to those involved. Highlight how that interaction creates a positive ripple in the room, which benefits all of us together. Ask students to tell what happened, who was involved, how it made them feel, or how it changed the outcome of the learning in a positive way. Give some snaps, do a cheer, whatever your favorite way to praise the room—authenticity is important. Although you may have noticed the moment and you are directing the discussion, allow students to share in the majority of the discussion. We are looking for buy-in and authentic moments.

Workstations are for applying the learning students have already been exposed to through mini-lessons and small-group lessons. Not every station will be graded or used as a measure for independent practice. Under the umbrella term of guided math, the purpose of a workstation is to allow students to practice and apply the skills they are acquiring in many formats and modalities. This is why the group dynamic is so powerful. It is meant to be a shared experience. There is an exception to the group work rule in my classroom. In order to take grades and allow time to have students think and process independently, I also have at least one workstation where students work independently. In this situation, they follow the rules and procedures for completing work apart from others. This allows a true measure of how they have synthesized the information.

Although there are challenges with grouping students, the benefits of this structure make it an effective experience for students and a vital part of an amplified math block. There's always a need for developing social skills, self-management, and leadership qualities in our students. Learning groups also allow students to work with diverse perspectives while helping develop adaptive reasoning. When anyone enters the classroom, will they take notice of students encouraging, supporting, sharing, and working side by side?

MANAGING CONTENT BALANCE

The management system is the foundation of the routine of our math block. Next, though, we need to layer the content students will interact with for their workstations. Once we have taught routines and expectations, the only new information students must take on from week to week is the actual content within that learned routine. This ensures that we have created a calm, clear foundation for students to seize learning opportunities. Once students know the structure is going to be the same today, tomorrow, and next week, they can relax and absorb new content without distraction.

Once we have put time and energy into creating the best, most AMPED structure for our math block, it is just as vital to pour high-quality relevant, meaningful, and engaging content into this structure. When choosing the content we put out, we want to keep things familiar yet fresh. For example, we may have familiarized students with the procedure for a math hunt activity, having done one for adding fractions. So, we can use the math hunt format to work on decimals standards next. This procedure can later become subtracting, then measuring, then comparing, and so on. The same iteration can take place with math journaling or any other task with which students are comfortable.

The goal of creating a familiar structure and providing fresh content is to differentiate students' learning in workstations. In this way, workstations can serve as "familiar but fresh" review, affirming students by meeting them where their knowledge bank rests. We can keep workstations fresh, though, by inspiring students to strategize, conceptualize, and problem-solve through related, high-interest activities.

In a traditional classroom setting, teachers often do much of the work, either by lecturing the whole period or providing all the answers too soon and too quickly, which in some way deprives students of their opportunity to explore on their own. In this pattern, students become passive receivers of knowledge, relying mainly on teachers for information. In addition, they seldom have the opportunity to work with other people in groups and consequently fail to practice cooperative learning, causing learned dependence. This certainly cultivates familiarity; however, it's anything but fresh.

If we desire our learners to behave differently, they should go beyond being dependent on someone to feed them knowledge. They need to spend time working on their own both in partners and in groups. In view of the significance of learner autonomy, students need time in practice to become proficient. Among ways of facilitating learner independence, workstations seem to help students learn by themselves and encourage them to take part in learning with group members. Workstations can improve students' learning motivation, putting the student into an active participant role rather than a passive receiver of information.

MANAGEMENT THROUGH MEANINGFUL CHOICES

The hard work of management is in the launch of your system and expectations. The exciting part is in keeping math workstations full of wonder and engagement. This is a key factor in the balanced, AMPED math block. Student engagement creates autonomy; a productive hum takes over as students actively participate in meaningful math practices. Although not every lesson will realistically have a low floor and high ceiling, we want to strive to affirm, inspire, and challenge students through what we ask them to do. Naturally, activities will inspire students differently. Giving students meaningful choices is one important tool for fostering students' self-motivated inspiration.

One rule of thumb in any arrangement of workstation choices is to put a limit on the number of students who can be at one station at any given time. This eliminates overcrowding. In a rotation system, this isn't an issue because student groups travel through stations for a set number of minutes and rotate at the sound of a timer for each station. When implementing the self-paced management system, however, stipulations about doing all activities once before repeating activities, and the number of students allowed per activity, will need to be established first.

When I first started out with guided math, I took a good hard look at the activities I was putting out for students. The majority of these so-called workstations were partner activities created with the intent of practicing content in a game context. Now, mind you, this was over a decade ago. The guided math structure has undoubtedly evolved, and with it the resources and research on effective math instruction. I am not saying a partner game is not a valid station choice, but it certainly should not be the only workstation option.

As I thought about my challenging students, I grew anxious thinking about the high number of bodies I had in the room with the limited number of resources at my fingertips. I needed to calm the chaos, so I began formulating a whole new type of math experience. I wanted to build a well-rounded math student. I wanted students to have meaningful choices that furthered their math thinking; I also had to make the best use of my time and resources with so many bodies in the room.

With all of these factors at play, I created Math STACK™, an acronym for designing flexible workstations that create a well-rounded math experience. I share this acronym with the hope that it may be able to help give you stability, but I caution you *not* to adopt this acronym simply because it is in this book! Making meaningful choices for your workstations is something that is personal and specific. While acronyms are always fun, they should not overrule the best choices for your students. A simple numbered list can be how students move through choices.

As I share STACK™ with you, think about how you can make it your own. I highly suggest taking parts of STACK™ that speak to you while also being open to incorporating what works well for your students *apart* from the acronym. Feel free to create a new acronym with your last name, school mascot, grade level, or heaven forbid, not use an acronym at all! Surprisingly enough, you don't have to have an acronym to run an exceptional math block!

As acronyms go, each letter in the word STACK™ stands for a workstation activity that students visit in our rotation system. *S* stands for "small group." A teacher-led small group is where students visit me to get an intensive, differentiated lesson on the new content. All of my small-group lessons have the same objective, but differentiation comes into play in terms of how we work toward our goal. Which strategies do we use? What number range is best for each group? Should we use the concrete, pictorial, or abstract? No matter what grade level I teach, I make it a point to see every student in a small group daily or almost daily. This requires a strict use of time and pacing. For some, this might not yet be attainable, and that's ok. How often can you see students, and how can you pace that out over the week?

The *T* in STACK™ stands for "technology"—math on a device. How this plays out is something that will vary from grade level to grade level, but I like a combination of math fact practice and app-type gameplay that reinforces math concepts in a fun way. Some schools purchase web-based programs that track students, and some do not. The technology station is something that continues to change based on new and exciting programs and apps that emerge each year. Consistently, this is a station that students greatly enjoy.

With a technology station, it can be helpful to designate devices to students for ease of logging in or having what is needed on specific technology for those students. Different colored mouse pads, tablet covers, or a number on the home screen can be easy ways to establish which device students work with. If anything becomes difficult with this station, such as logging in or knowing how to access the activities needed, I designate students who are gifted in the area of technology and who love the task to be the tech expert in the room.

A stands for "application." This station closely follows what we are doing in our small-group lessons but lags behind a day or two or three. I do this with intent because some students visit this station before meeting with me in their small-group time. I want students to have an opportunity to be comfortable with the new learning before I expect them to work independently. Typically, this station is done with the student working in the room independently and then placing the work in their folder for check-in I take a grade on the application station most often because it is a measurable skill practice-type activity. However, there are times when I will have students check answers with a buddy from the group or with an answer key. Those days, the station is more about allowing students to self-regulate and correct their procedures.

The general idea with the application station is that students will be completing an independent practice activity. When I have a great developmental disparity in my students' academic readiness, I differentiate the choice into two or three buckets or drawers: on level, remediation, and enrichment. Students are assigned a particular drawer or bucket from which to pull their activity, ensuring they get a good fit for their ability level. There is no stigma or label in this system. It is simply where they pull the activities. This differentiation technique applies to all stations. This ensures that students are able to receive the practice and application on the skills that are most important and powerful in their journey as a growing mathematician.

The C in STACK™ stands for "creating math." Creating math is done in a math journal. The creating-math station can look many ways based on how you want to have students work in their journals. My main criteria are that I provide a lot of variety and structure. Students have a structured assignment for creating math in their journal rather than it being used in a traditional sense as just a response tool. Examples of what we may do in a week in our math journal are graphic organizers, math sorts, word problems, cut-and-paste activities, and answer flaps. Occasionally, using colored paper is a simple way to add interest. Creating math in a journal is a way for students to keep an authentic record of math learning. Students use these as a learning reference to past concepts as we spiral review through the school year.

Depending on the grade level, the journal will take on different roles. For lower-elementary students, the journal is a place to keep math learning. The station, by contrast, is interactive, with simple sorts, questions and answers, colored-paper activities, and response to learning. These base activities are first taught in the whole-group setting before becoming station activities, as there are a lot of habits and expectations to put into place.

For older students, creating math can be done as a note-taking record of math learning that takes place during the mini-lesson as well as the application level of working through actual problems. I used to combine both of these in the same journal, but in later years I found that I enjoyed having one note-taking journal or composition book for mini-lessons in the whole-group setting paired with a station journal for the day-to-day assignments where students applied the learning. Students have an easier time referencing their notes this way, and it seemed a better experience for them overall. When I need to check their work, it was easier to navigate this way as well.

I find that students need many examples of activity- or paper-formatting and excellent work up front to rise to the expectation. One way I do this is to keep a teacher example journal. The example journal I have contains the formatting for the activities without any answers. Students can reference the example journal during a workstation for ideas on how to organize or create the response. This eliminates unnecessary interruptions for non-content related needs.

Although I love the math journal station, I did not anticipate how much my students would love it as well. They take pride in their journals and consistently want to show them to visitors in the room—no matter the age of the student. If math journals are not for you, how could you use the C for creating math in another way? It's a relatively open-ended part of the acronym!

The final letter in the acronym of STACK™ is *K*, which stands for "kinesthetic." The kinesthetic station allows students to work hands-on. Hands-on work can be playing a partner or group game; matching questions and answers; or going on a math hunt around the room with cards, pocket charts, and hands-on pieces and parts for math exploration. No matter the age of the math student, this station is a favorite. Age-appropriate math tasks appeal to all ages. Students experience math in a way that may require more interaction and movement than the other workstations. Just like the other stations, variety keeps this station engaging, so it's a great opportunity for including high-quality, spiraled review activities in many formats.

As we devise choices for our students to make, we want to consider whether we are exposing them to many formats and modalities. Are we creating interest, engagement, and meaning, or simply putting something out to keep them occupied? One of the most significant issues we come across is maintaining attention and high-quality work during workstations. There's a good chance this was something you wrote down over the course of the attention activities in the last chapter. For me, keeping students motivated and excited to go to workstations is done through careful planning and thought up front.

MANAGING MOTIVATION

The long-standing traditional math format has been to state a rule, show an example of the rule, and have students practice the rule. The end. What an incredible contrast we can offer students in the guided math structure. With guided math, multifaceted, meaningful math moments are embedded in a math block centered around creating empowered mathematicians.

In the workstation structure, we can create collaborative learning moments for our students through purposeful math practice. Just like we make an effort to relate to student interests in our other lessons, we want to do the same in our workstation choices. Toward that end, I find myself continually asking, "What can I do to motivate students in this math moment I have created?" Although it is not realistic that I will always have fun props and pop-culture tie-ins to all workstation choices, I can certainly sprinkle in the novelty!

How can I inspire a love of learning through matching interests and math? As you collect and use moments of inspiration, you'll begin to accumulate a bank of resources that motivates your learners and excites them to stay more focused and produce high-quality work. In my experience, most students notice and appreciate when extra effort goes into the choices we provide. But our gestures need not be grand! Simply using colored or decorative paper while prepping student materials can infuse a little special touch during workstations. Providing different ways to respond during workstations, such as write-and-wipe plastic sleeves with dry-erase markers, can also be a simple motivator for students. It's always fun to use themed math tie-ins for science and social studies topics, seasonal topics, and anything else of interest to your students.

Just as we want students to put forth an effort, we can model the same energy through our thoughtful consideration of meaningful choices fueled by motivators for our students. When students love what they are doing, the result is engagement! I add special touches to the areas where I notice any downtrend in participation and engagement. Even a change in the color of a tray or bucket to tie in to something going on seasonally will create interest. These efforts are greatly appreciated by students. Start small. This insight goes back to staying alert and giving attention to our math block throughout the year. These meaningful choices help create an amplified math block.

MANAGING EVALUATION

You've gotten workstations launched and running, student engagement and enthusiasm is palpable, and you are beginning to feel those top-of-the-mountain guided math gains. Then, before you can run next door to share your math bliss with your teacher BFF, the student work piles overwhelmingly begin coming in. Rather than one traditional math assignment for the day, you now have up to six math experiences to track and check per student every day. Heaps of recording sheets, journal entries, exit tickets, independent skill pages, and digital check-ins all threaten to steal your evenings for the next 180 days. I am holding my breath in stressful angst just reliving it.

There's an easy solution of balanced accountability lurking in those piles of work that is both fastidious enough to inspire student effort yet fair on your time and workload as a teacher. Depending on grade level and grading requirements, you can create a system for accountability that reflects a high-quality standard but still allows us grace in the face of these heaps.

First, the teacher-led small group spearheads the accountability plan. The consistent face-to-face time with students allows me to know students on a much deeper math level than the whole-group model has in years past. Daily, I watch students use strategies, listen to them explain and justify their thinking, and see them process through the content presented. Teacher-led small group is literally formative assessment in math moments. Here, I create anecdotal notes of strengths, gaps, strategies, and enrichment for students as needed. With this baseline of knowledge, I determine what workstation accountability will round out the full picture of how my mathematicians are performing.

What has worked for me is to have Thursdays be the main accountability day. That day of the week is what works for me and helps me get my act together so things can be adjusted on Friday by the students. For me, here's what that entails: At the end of the day on Thursdays, students take out their math folders containing all recording sheets, scratch paper, and independent practice—any and all paperwork collected during the week of workstations. They also take out their math journals and open to the area where we began the week. This is something I choose to incorporate, but it is not a requirement for everyone running guided math in their classrooms. I have already determined the two to three assignments from which I am taking a grade for the week. After students have left, I collect those items or grade them on the spot.

Once I determine which two or three assignments I am grading for Monday through Thursday, I then put the remaining work into two piles: essential and nonessential. The nonessentials will go into the recycle bin. These are nonessentials that confuse parents when sent home: half-filled recording sheets because I assigned only half the problems, or scratch paper that looks a mess and holds no value for review or reteaching. A nonessential paper is where the value was in the moment of the math experience rather than in the result-ing notes. Some weeks I find that we have more non-essentials than others. It used to bother me when I would have a week with little to "show" for it, but when pondering the actual math experiences, I knew it was nothing to hold guilt over.

The essential work is spot-checked for completion, accuracy, and quality control. You determine the standard for that, but this is where you will teach yourself to glance for a pattern of proven accu-racy rather than evaluate and appraise each written numeral. I know this isn't rocket science, but it deserves mentioning because many teachers are convinced they need to grade all work and somehow feel less-than when something slips by.

When I am scanning the essential pile, I am also looking for high-quality work to highlight in a praise report that sets expecta-tions. This is a treasure and not taken lightly, so I try to make sure

I highlight everyone if humanly possible before making a second round. If something really stands out, I grab it and snap the picture to be used when the time is right. The reason this is such an effective practice is that, in time, everyone gets to be recognized for special effort. Sometimes it's neatness, other times it's carrying out intricate steps on scratch paper—any special effort that raises the bar on quality work.

For older students, adding a fun superlative or taking it to the next level for students as they are recognized continues to draw students in to listen to the praise. This was something I learned from one of my children's high school teachers. Not only did he share superlatives up on the board for the entire day but he would also write it on a Post-it note for that student and leave it on their desk. They carried those Post-its inside their phone cases for the year. *Treasured.*

These quality control moments are not done daily, or they would become less than sincere. With praise and reflection, we want to keep things authentic so there's no pressure to keep up with this in a daily schedule. When these praise reports happen, I like having the work or a picture up when students walk into the room. They will begin analyzing whose it is or why it was highlighted. The same goes for students as they clean up workstations to gather for the closing reflection. Just quietly putting the picture up will initiate student discussions.

Refrain from the temptation to "fix a problem" with this same method of highlighting it. If something is negative and needs to be fixed, discuss it with those involved in a private setting. We don't want to shame students publicly; it will create a divide and broken trust. If we continue our conversations with students, partners, and groups naturally, then we can address issues this way.

Now if the issue is just a pattern of pencils on the floor, dangling headphones, or the like, we can take a picture of this kind of issue to say, "Hey! What's going on here? This station can close, or we can fix it." That's not going to individually shame anyone yet can draw attention to a problem we need to be addressed by the entire class.

As you conduct the guided math structure, you will ebb and flow through maximum management and management mayhem. Circle back to attention when you find consistent breakdowns and keep addressing concerns with students through meaningful discussions, tighter restrictions, or a change in how something is structured. For example, if students are allowed to use a certain area of the classroom for a workstation but trouble tends to erupt in off-task behavior or incomplete work, it's ok to close that privilege and have students sit at their tables until they earn that back. Ultimately the formula for success for any management mayhem, big or small, is attention and adjustment. Many times, small problems can be adjusted quickly so they lose steam and don't become a larger issue.

The responsibility of management is very much in the control of the educator creating the experience. Managing the workstation time in the math block usually revolves around pacing to the natural stamina of the class while providing both meaningful and engaging materials that are also developmentally appropriate for the academic level of the learners. When students are enticed with quality work that makes sense to their skill level and have just enough time to work to their best ability by staying on task, they have the highest chance of meeting expectations.

CHAPTER 4

PURPOSE:
POSITIONING LEARNING

An essential part of AMPED teaching is creating an environment that promotes opportunities for learning. Guided math, as a learning structure, inherently does this but it's still important to consider how we can further present mathematically rich moments for students beyond the baseline of guided math.

As a person who labored through math myself, I know first-hand how important it is to provide a strong foundation in math that marries both conceptual and procedural understanding, but let's dive further into what we know about effective math instruction. From addition to algorithms, there are ways to expose students to high-quality mathematical opportunities. Regardless of curriculum, there are exciting practices we can put into place to unlock mathematical understanding in our students.

So, how do we position learning in order to ensure student success? First, we want to be as explicit as we can in our teaching when we model a concept, strategy, or procedure. Then, we need to pair explicit teaching with modeled math thinking. Verbalizing each thought as we explicitly teach gives students a true understanding of how a mathematician processes through a problem.

In doing these two things to start, students are given a clear picture of both a concept being taught and the thinking involved in its process. Making sense of math instruction is much of the battle. Consider that many of our own math struggles occur when we try to work a problem, get stuck, begin guessing, and find ourselves unsure of how to move forward. Use that experience to model the process of working through these moments of difficulty, not only modeling the perfect process but also sharing the part of the process that you consider a misstep *before* working your way through it. With this modeling in place, there is no guessing left for the student to struggle with when working on the problems later. Explicit instruction and modeled thinking help all students make sense of the varied skills and concepts they will encounter through the year.

The next step in positioning the learning is to follow up with visual representation through the use of manipulatives, a graphic organizer, or a sketch of the information in a problem. When we provide a visual representation, we need to tie it back to conceptual understanding. As an example, many students who struggle with computation will remain stuck and anxious about how we arrived at the number twenty-three in the first step and will be unable to keep listening to the steps as we continue through a problem. The twenty-three in the first step was nothing the teacher focused on because it wasn't new learning. Had the teacher taken a moment and done a quick sketch of the computation to arrive at twenty-three off to the side of the problem, it could have created a scaffold in the learning for those not yet confident in computation. Everyone benefits from these mathematical teaching practices, including students who have language barriers, working-memory issues, or gaps in their education experience, and students who have had all learning opportunities awarded to them in life.

The next way to position learning is to show students how to observe and use patterns. Recognizing patterns is a major part in realizing how to strategize and solve problems, yet we rarely tell students this explicitly. Patterns are found in how problems are set up, written out, and carried out to completion. We can teach students to recognize these patterns by simply noticing and verbalizing them. A great place to start finding patterns is examining how word problems are set up. Keywords, knowing what to solve for, and the setup of information all follow patterns based on the type of word problem. We can distinguish this type or that type of word problem by analyzing the makeup of the problems themselves.

The final step in positioning learning involves intentionally creating a forum of communication in your environment that allows students to have meaningful discussions that promote positive learning traits. With the purpose of instilling adaptive reasoning into our mathematicians, we encourage explanations, justifications, and logical thought processes as part of working through problems. As part of the math warm-up and in the mini-lesson, students listen to peers create a plan, name strategies, mentally process out loud, and carry out procedures. It then carries over into the discussions at workstations and in teacher-led small groups as well. These small practices that we encourage and model daily produce a productive disposition toward math learning. Students believe in their abilities and efficacy as mathematicians, seeing math as a useful and worthwhile endeavor.

AMPED MINI-LESSONS

Because they require addressing learners of various levels, mini-lessons require a lot of intention in order to be effective and inclusive. This does not mean our mini-lessons become long and involved. Back in chapter 1, we discussed the importance of bridging old and new concepts in order to bring all students to the table. To further clarify the purpose of a mini-lesson, let's break our mini-lessons into three categories of math proficiency: conceptual learning, strategies for solving, and procedural learning. Categorizing mini-lessons creates an organized pattern of teaching, which gives structure to how to present the information. This clear focus gives us a succinct goal or purpose for the dynamic mini-lesson.

If I am focusing on conceptual learning, my goal is on building understanding around the learning objective or what I like to call my "priority skill." In a conceptual lesson, I am not focused on numbers and problem-solving but more on the big picture of the idea in general. One way to build conceptual learning is by showing how this new topic, skill, or math concept relates to the world around me. So, I share how it relates to our lives, where I may see it or use it, and any connection to it that builds that understanding. It may be that I explain a role that something has within a more complex structure, such as how the equal sign is part of an algebraic equation and its function in that formula. Nevertheless, I focus on bringing understanding and not computing. Conceptual learning fills in the fundamental knowledge and big ideas of a concept.

In conceptual learning, we use a line of questioning that asks students to philosophize on the topic. Some common prompts for conceptual learning include:

- Estimate the time it would take . . .
- Is it reasonable to say that . . .
- If I were going to solve this problem mentally, what would I need to know?
- Which of these two fractions is the smaller one?
- Why do you believe this to be true?
- Explain how you would determine the value of . . .
- Find the similarity between . . .

To use an analogy, conceptual understanding is your grandfather telling you about a project and the tools he will use to complete it. Procedural understanding begins when he grabs the correct tool from the toolbox and begins actually working on the project. We want to foster knowledge both of *what* we are learning and *how* we will work through it while carrying out the steps for finding a solution.

For example, if I am teaching coin values for the first time to a group of young students, I want to access their cognitive structure—their sense of what is already familiar—and then build upon what they have been exposed to that relates to this new learning. So, I might use snap cubes as a way to show the value of the coins. For a penny, I use one snap cube because my students have been exposed to the idea of a single unit and have an understanding of the value of one snap cube through number sense. When I show a nickel, students see five snap cubes, a dime is a tower of ten snap cubes, and finally, a quarter is twenty-five snap cubes arranged in two towers of ten and a tower of five. Not only do my students understand the value of a quarter through the use of twenty-five snap cubes, but they also recognize the value of a quarter as two dimes and one nickel because of the consistent conceptual model I am using to explain this.

Similarly, I can create a real-life issue in our classroom that helps students distinguish area from perimeter. So, I can explain how I just purchased a new rug, and now I am not sure if it will fit in the space of our classroom. I can relate conceptually with my students in the real world, explaining the problem and the need for a solution that would measure the area and perimeter of both the room and the new rug. As we work through this problem, we are focused not on the answer but on the *process* I would set up for ensuring I could determine the answer. What would I need to know? How would I find out the information that I need? I am purposefully making connections to area and perimeter and building a foundation of understanding the difference.

The second category of math mini-lesson is strategies for solving. Part of conceptualizing is determining all of the factors that will play a part in the process of solving. One of those factors is picking a strategy for solving a problem. For example, in computation, multiple strategies can be applied, which then lead to specific steps for solving.

For example, if a student is solving a multiplication problem using the approach of an open number line, their process in solving will vary greatly from that of a student using a standard algorithm to solve, one using partial products to solve, or one using an area model, yet all will result in the same answer. Exploring strategic options creates adaptive reasoning in our students. If students can solve multiplication problems using many varied strategies, they can also connect the relationship of the numbers and how they change when multiplied.

The foundation of students' math understanding becomes multi-faceted when we emphasize strategies for solving in our math mini-lessons. This is a stark contrast to learning only a standard algorithm or strictly memorizing facts. While it is important to quickly recall facts and use a standard algorithm, those two methods only serve to help students answer basic, test-type, surface-level problems. True math understanding should promote wondering, pondering, and exploring. Can the student think critically about the skills we teach? How many strategies for solving can we explore to create a full understanding of the math concept?

In its basic form, a strategy-for-solving mini-lesson focuses on the strategy to be taught. When teaching a strategy lesson, we discuss how and why we use a strategy. In my class we name it and claim it. My goal is for students to be able to communicate their understanding. I want them to be able to state why we select a strategy, name the strategy, and tell how to carry it out *before* ever actually working through the procedure. For that reason, everything gets named, from filling a ten frame to count to ten, to counting on from the larger number in basic addition, to using strip diagrams or related facts. Many times, we don't think of these as strategies, but they absolutely are.

As students internalize these methods as strategies, they are empowered. They know they have a bank of ways to work with numbers. I create strategy visual cards we can put on a math focus wall once a strategy has been introduced. For the math mini-lesson, everyone is exposed to a general bank of important strategies related to our content in that grade level. These general and most used math strategies are introduced in the math mini-lessons while we are in the whole-group setting. Students can then refer to them throughout the different components of their math block.

Other strategies for solving will only be introduced during small groups with the students who specifically need them to be successful. These are typically reserved for two situations. First, we might introduce strategies for solving during small group as a way to offer students additional support when they are struggling. An example of this would be a chart that students need to reference to work through a step in order to recall information. This can also be something like using a number line with specific number ranges to compute because the student has not yet made the connection in less supportive ways. These support-based strategies are there to scaffold the student through the process in order to be successful. The ultimate goal is that, over time, these students will develop connections to move on to less supportive methods. This is done by weaning them from these strategies when the time is right.

Second, we might emphasize strategies for solving during small group when such strategies will take a student into more complex and challenging math concepts. Such strategies are explored *just* with the specific groups of students who exhibit the need for incremental mastery of complex competencies.

The third category of math mini-lesson is procedural learning. This is when we explicitly teach the steps necessary to carry out math problem-solving. Procedural learning is a step-by-step, problem-solving type of math lesson that should come *only after* conceptual understanding has been taught. This type of procedural math is what we traditionally think of when we remember enduring a textbook-type of math resource adoption, either as a student or as the teacher. We would turn the page and see at the top an example problem and the steps written out underneath it. Typically, workbooks were accompanied by the teacher at the front of the room talking through the steps.

While this approach might seem outdated in the context of AMPED guided math, procedural math can still be engaging! The thrill of solving new and more complex math concepts can be invigorating, and we want to be sure to create an engaging environment and culture in our lessons. However, we also need to be sure to also take the step of connecting conceptual learning and procedural learning. This allows students to think about their own thinking as they work critically. They will discover how they process like a mathematician by asking themselves questions like "Does my answer make sense?" and "Did I answer the question?"

No matter which category of mini-lesson we teach in guided math, the primary consideration is that not every student will be able to understand this new information in one sitting of the whole group. For some, it is going to take many exposures and formats to reinforce learning. Remember that reinforcement is part of the added value of small groups and workstations. In the mini-lesson itself, though, it is vital to mentally note those who may need this reinforcement while still staying on track with pacing for the rest of the students.

Too often, struggling students fall further and further behind because their lack of understanding of prior content prevents them from learning new material. This is a difficult cycle to break. But by devoting regular instructional time to reviewing and remediating past material, and by altering the ways the new material is presented so that it's more approachable for struggling students, we can increase the chances that these students will gradually find a more stable foothold in math and begin the difficult climb back to full understanding. When it comes to the current material, recognize that it may be necessary in the short term to modify the complexity of the new content so that it's approachable for all students. This way struggling students can begin to grasp the important ideas of the new material without being held back by their fragile understanding of the "old" material.

BUILDING INTEGRAL EXPERIENCES

The entire structure of guided math is about creating a well-rounded math student through integral experiences. Here, we can break that concept down a little more to really see how these experiences take place, then we can discuss how to amplify these experiences moving forward.

Each of us, with our grade-level expectations and given or purchased resources, becomes a lesson designer of sorts. We want to integrate hands-on learning, skill application, and positive social experiences throughout our daily math activities. This is a big responsibility, but considering that we run a math block for 180 days, it is important that we really think about how we are choosing the student work and guided math components that create a well-rounded math experience. Integral experiences go beyond acronyms, like STACK™, or structures, like guided math. Whether we see two, three, four, or five groups in a day is not the focus. What really matters are the substantive math experiences and interactions that make up those instructional rounds for students. At base, then, integral learning needs to be meaningful. In the context of mathematics, the idea of making meaning might be hard to grasp, so let's step back and consider what meaningful learning looks like in another domain: reading.

In the third year of my teaching career, I had a student from Japan enter my classroom. After two weeks of instruction, he was reading full pages of English text. At first, I believed this was a result of my excellent reading instruction. Ahem . . . no. He would look up after reading the entire page of his reader with a blank look on his face. There was no actual understanding. His incredible reading ability was a result of the memorization of sounds. He had no idea of the meaning of what he had just decoded. The running record indicated that he was a fluent and accurate reader. I knew better.

At this time, our school had a high ELL population. In fact, 95 percent of my class was made up of students who did not speak English at home. The school adopted a small-group reading approach, and we heavily used phonics for our reading instruction. The result was that students could read fluently and accurately in a phonics-based reader but had little to no comprehension of what they beautifully read. Sight word–based books were impossible for my students and brought a harsh light to the truth. The phonics-only reading approach ultimately had to go. Don't get me wrong, I believe in phonics instruction and it has always been an important focus for me with all students, ELL or not. But it can't be the only instructional experience. It's a part of the whole experience. Meaning over memorization.

People often don't think of the importance of meaningful learning when it comes to math, but to children, many mathematical concepts can be equally meaningless without a concrete resource or picture to go with it. Simply teaching formulas and steps to solve abstract problems creates students who don't know what they don't know. As a result, students can't think critically about what they are doing because they don't have any meaning or concept of what they are solving. They don't care about math or feel empowered by it. They simply know of it as a page of problems to solve to earn a grade.

Integral math experiences cover standards-based content while engaging and empowering students to apply the learning in meaningful ways. Meaningful math involves exploration, sense-making, and reasoning. In the process, students engage in a strategy or approach and begin to solve problems. Along the way, they either realize that their initial beliefs are correct or find a new approach for a better outcome.

The excitement in mathematics happens in problem-solving. This involves asking, "Is my line of thinking going to work out?" or "Did I reason correctly?" Just putting out a page of problems day after day is arithmetic rather than mathematics. Arithmetic lacks ideas, concepts, understandings, and connections. When students only follow steps or memorize facts without also having time to work on sense-making and reasoning through problems, the meaning of mathematics becomes lost. When that meaning is lost, connection and engagement fade.

While it is important to consider a variety of meaningful math explorations during our math block in order to create integral experiences, it is also crucial to keep workstations about the application of learned content. A big disconnect I have witnessed, time and time again, occurs when students walk up to a workstation with anticipation only to find a worksheet on a skill in a format they do not recognize or understand. Students sit in anxious, unproductive frustration. When we throw something in a workstation just to keep our students busy, we create negative math experiences. To amplify the workstation experience, we want to be sure to pique interest and provide application-level work on the targeted levels of the content we have taught.

Workstations are like a palette for the artist to paint with. What we choose to put into workstations creates the bank of what the mathematician can practice and apply. Like the math warm-up, workstations are a spiraled review of previously learned material. Ideally, workstations include a variety of skills from as current as yesterday to four months ago. The idea is for students to become comfortable, automatic, and accurate as they practice and apply older learning and newer learning together. Making these important connections as students mathematically mature over the course of the year cements the learning into a powerful math foundation.

FILLING MATHEMATICAL GAPS

The reality is that every student has mathematical gaps accrued through their school career. Learning gaps occur for all kinds of reasons: student or teacher illness, family circumstance, inadequate teaching of a topic, curriculum didn't go into depth, pacing of the math lesson, pacing of the year's content, learning difficulties, language barriers, a pandemic . . . I digress. In the world we live in, our students will come to us with mathematical gaps.

My daughter, a college student, tackled Calculus 3 her freshman year. Now in her junior year of a science major, I frequently see her working through a screen full of formulas with both numbers and Greek letters. Recently, my daughter was home on a school break. Together we sat in my office as I worked on a fifth-grade math resource and she revised her genetics research project. As I worked through an answer key on multiplication, my daughter stared at my screen and said, "I don't solve it that way," referring to the multiplication problems on the screen. I showed her the multiple methods used to solve for multiplication, which typically begin in second grade and build to this resource in fifth grade. She began to get flustered and explained that I couldn't be right. She stopped and stared, following the simple path for solving and then shouted, "I didn't know zeroes could be so important!" Then she worked each problem out in her own way. This is a Gen Z student who was immersed in "new" math instruction under my careful eye throughout her school career. She rarely missed a day of school, and I valued all of her teachers. By my watch, she should have no mathematical gaps. How could she handle so many complex formulas and courses without these basic computation procedures? This budding genetic scientist did not have exposure to standard algorithms, area models, or partial products when multiplying. When she saw the standard algorithm, she said, "Why didn't I know this!? Can it really be that easy?" When I asked her to tell me what she did to multiply large numbers together, she began reciting multiples in strings and then something about a goose egg . . . there was some touch math from the early 2000s in there, too. We spent a few minutes reviewing the new strategies on my screen together in a quiet shock. Ultimately, she was just disappointed that she missed strategies that would simplify the process for her.

The point of sharing this experience is that every student from every background will be exposed to different methods, strategies, techniques, or lack of, for solving in their unique school career. If we assume they got it last year or three years ago, we miss out on important moments of learning that can be the difference between a student loving math and feeling successful or the opposite.

Workstations are a wonderful time to fill in these learning gaps when we put out activities to refresh, review, and revisit topics. One of the best ways I have found to fill in gaps for struggling mathematicians during workstations is to plan ahead by putting out the foundational skills related to upcoming units rather than waiting for students to fail and then trying to catch them up when the unit is over.

As humans, when we are given a new task or walk into an unfamiliar task, we ask ourselves three questions subconsciously: How do I feel about this? Do I possess the skills to do this? Does it interest me? This process of self-doubt is something we witness in our students. If we can anticipate the pushback against something difficult that we know is coming up for students, we can pivot and put a spin on how to present the information. By keeping these same three questions in mind as we build out our math block, we can learn how to create an inviting routine.

EYES ON THE PRIZE

Am I inspired daily with epic content at my fingertips? No. Let's be real here. The best way I have combated the struggle of refilling my workstations is to front-load the content for myself. I have to put time and attention into workstations. The first year we take on workstations is an uphill climb as we put a tremendous amount of thought and prep into providing meaningful experiences for our students. I tend to create, prep, and build my bank of resources during my off-teaching times. I know people have strong feelings about using rest time to work, but this is my personal experience. Putting in the time and prep for a few summer days means that I get to leave school on time, which adds up to more rest when I need it most. This strategy means that I don't have to experience the stress of worrying about switching out workstations when I am in the throes of weekly lesson prep.

As a teacher who unrolled and cut out miles of lamination and bought out the tubs, buckets, and plastic bags of the dollar stores in my area, it is important to validate the work involved in creating a bank of resources. The guided math structure and components require more prep time and materials in the initial stages of implementation than a traditional math block taught mainly in the abstract format through procedural lessons. The well-worth-it payoff comes when you can pull from a bank of rich, well-loved resources covering many levels of understanding through the content topics all year. The joy and excitement for the next topic is met by simply grabbing the next week's resources and putting them out. This is something I did on Friday afternoons with the help of Sammy Sorts-a-Lot and Olivia the Organizer. These two student types eagerly came over to my table during the last half hour of the day on Fridays asking if they could change out stations for me. Yes. You. May.

When visitors come to my classroom, it is difficult not to brag over . . . ahem, *share* my library of math workstations and lesson activities. I often am asked how to best organize workstations. I have found that content topics make the most sense when I want to find a specific station activity. For this reason, I put them into boxes by topic. I also have some special seasonal workstations that, although they have different topics, get put together because they all come out during a certain month of the school year. This is of course a personal choice, so the main criteria is that the system has to work for how you tend to use materials in your room. For me, I wanted to be able to change out stations for the next week by pulling by topic and grabbing those baggies from the bins of topics to put out.

It's important to take stock of what you create, prep, or accumulate for your workstations over the years and align it to the content students are working through. Through the years, I have experienced the research-based directive that workstations are best for students as a spiral review of previously learned content. When I expect students to work independently of my instruction while also carrying out collaborative interactions with group mates or partners, I want the content to be thought-provoking but not new.

I keep workstations for remediation, on-level work, and enrichment. When starting out, this is not realistic or expected, so it is ok to work with the resources you have while building up your library.

Family members, room moms, and school volunteers all had a hand in helping me create workstations. As a teaching team, we would also divide the standards and each be responsible for finding and prepping a portion. This was helpful when starting out. Sometimes I even sent a roll of laminated stations with a box of plastic baggies home in a backpack to have them cut out and returned a week later.

Laminated station activities are certainly not the only way to address workstations. In fact, it is just how I address the *K* (kinesthetic) in the Math STACK™ acronym. Another way I have created integral experiences to amplify workstations is to take the content that I have in a worksheet or textbook and transform it. Can I take ten problems from a skill page and turn them into a math puzzle? Can I take those same problems and make them the basis for a hunt around the room for answers? How about adapting those problems by integrating them into current events or trends that my students can't get enough of? Put student names into your problems and watch them smile and giggle as they work. Once I make these templates, I can change out the content. When we show students that we are putting effort in and making it personal and meaningful, the result is a much more interested participant.

Pacing is also a crucial element for sustaining impactful, truly AMPED practices in the guided math block. Bad pacing can take all of our efforts toward effective teaching practices and render them null and void. It is crucial to monitor how your students are responding and interacting within the active lesson. We want to pace to their highest ability of absorption. Maximizing the minutes means being aware of potential pitfalls. If we push students too far out of their comfort range to take in new information, we can cloud the information or confuse them. We want to keep it concise. Make the best of the time allotted for the component you are teaching but be willing to stop rather than push too far.

Although I am sharing pacing pains as if we are all the type to become long winded and overteach, there are also some teachers who can be too concise and short in their math explanations. I actually find myself in this boat. I think part of this is due to teaching the same skills and concepts for so many years. We become so used to the information we are delivering that we forget how new and daunting it is to our learners. We graze over the surface expecting full understanding. It is important to scaffold the lessons to the learners they are meant for in the here and now. As much as you need to, remind yourself to see the day's objective from brand-new eyes. How would my students benefit best from learning the concept today? Teacher-led small-group time will open your eyes to areas where stronger teaching is necessary. As you notice trends or areas of disconnect and mistakes, adjust your pacing of those skills.

Overall, our teaching practices and the time we spend in the various components should be focused toward positioning the learning for the greatest gains. No matter how hard we try, we won't be perfect in our pacing or practices, but the goal is to continually try to improve every opportunity for learning for our students.

CHAPTER 5

EMPATHY:
EDUCATING WITH INTENTION

Every year of implementation of guided math, or any other structure applied to the learning day, will ebb and flow based on seasons, routines, management, a mixture of learning levels, personalities in the room, instructional practices, resources used, and any number of other factors. A constant in all of these variables is us. How will we navigate what we see and experience during these implemented structures? It's a normal tendency to compare one year to another, one class to another, one curriculum adoption to another, but many times, we are the dominating force in the sea of variables. We actually have a lot of control in how we run any structure. Yes, some years will be better or worse experiences for us. This is a fact. But we do have the ability to adjust and make positive changes and amplify all of the facets that create the math block experience. It's why you picked up this book!

Ultimately, an AMPED math block is more than the sum of its parts. Why? Because guided math allows you to be fully present; its structure gives you the flexibility to show up, each and every day, for your students as they learn and grow as mathematicians. Indeed, one of the major benefits of guided math is that it's designed for cultivating relationships: between student and teacher, student and student, and student and subject.

How, then, can you as an educator leverage the AMPED math block as a way to build those relationships in impactful ways? And, amidst all the explicit instruction and activities, how can you remain mindful of students' needs as mathematicians, individuals, and members of your classroom community? As an educator, you're likely already a deeply empathic person. But, if that capacity for understanding students isn't motivated toward real, actionable change—in process, in learning outcomes, and in relationships— then you might end up feeling like you're emotionally flailing. In this chapter, then, we'll explore several ways to leverage your intuition in mindful, purposeful ways. In particular, I'll highlight some ways to foster effective communication with your students—both as a speaker *and* a listener.

LISTENING INTENTLY

As teachers, we can pinpoint the millisecond that mayhem has the potential to erupt. It's our sixth sense that quickly develops as we take the helm of our first classroom of students. Educators are always ready to intervene and react to what we see or hear brewing in our classrooms. Survival, necessity, and instinct tell us how to listen to lead our students through the day. We are quick to interject and put things on track when we hear things going awry. This same capacity for responsive listening can be harnessed as a tremendous asset for AMPED math instruction. We will always listen to lead, but for the sake of amplifying our math instruction, we will listen to *understand* rather than to react.

Rather than jumping in to give insight or direct students on a task, AMPED listening begins by *just listening*—listening intently to the full student and classroom experience that is present. Listen with the focus of providing new or potential learning opportunities in the future. Listen with the purpose of providing future greatness. Listen to the natural reactions as students are presented with information. Listen to how students initiate conversations with learning partners or groups. Listen to how students navigate transitions. As you listen for understanding, taking on a more receptive role, you will discover ways to amplify your current routine. Rather than reacting in order to fix or change something, just let it sit and motivate you on rethinking how to create the best situation for the most students. When students have a chance to problem-solve or get through a situation, what steps do they naturally know to take? What step or steps could you add or address for them to help in the future?

During the first week of my first year of teaching, my administrator put an article in our boxes to be read. I tucked the paper article in my tote at the end of the day and diligently read it that evening, highlighter in hand. First-year teacher enthusiasm at its finest. I don't remember if the article was from an education journal or who the author was, but the general idea was to ask students how they came to an answer, not just when the answer was correct but, even more importantly, when the answer is incorrect. This idea stuck out to me because it was something I would never naturally do. My schooling experience led me to believe that the teacher always expects the correct answer; to be incorrect was to offer the wrong response. The classroom was where the teacher told us the right information and how to do it. We had to remember it and recite it to prove our intelligence. The teacher collected correct answers and seemed to secretly care more for those students who always had them.

The following week, my principal was doing a walk-through, and I called on a student who gave me an incorrect answer. My heart sank. This was over twenty-two years ago, and I can still vividly picture the child enthusiastically raising his hand wearing his gray T-shirt with a howling wolf. I can hear the hum of the AC unit, and I can feel my heart beating in my chest. This first-year teacher walk-through was as high stakes a moment as I had ever had in my life up to this point. In fact, I felt all of my years of college and training had led me to this moment. This was it. My first walk-through. I paused as I felt the presence of my administrator. I remembered the article. I scanned all of the eyes of my students landing on his eager eyes and carefully and slowly asked the student why he believed this answer to be true and could he please explain his thinking. My heart was audibly beating, and I felt both hot and cold at the same time.

In that moment, I felt like I had given away my power, and I hoped my administrator wouldn't see me as weak. The student's response was logical yet incorrect, and I understood how to help. The response opened a dialogue, allowing other students to relate, and it turned the lesson down a path I never imagined. I was uncomfortable, felt like I had failed, and my stomach was upset long after the administrator left the room. Later, though, I found a note from my administrator about how effective that moment was for the student and how terrific it was to see the opportunity taken.

That moment changed me as a teacher. It wasn't that it was difficult to make that shift in my natural tendency and in the privacy of my four walls, but the timing of the article and the pressure of the observation were the catalyst in making me take the leap. Even as I did it, I questioned it and I felt uncomfortable. My students likely felt the opposite. Perhaps it was the first time they thought, "She cares about our thinking. My wrong answer doesn't mean I am dumb. It means I got off track and other people do it, too."

Fortunately, in the two decades following that moment in my classroom, I continued to grow in my desire to understand and meet student needs. Although it can feel strange to try a new technique or allow for a different procedure, these impactful moments continue to push us in our craft. Educators grow and change for the better through our experiences, our colleagues, and by learning from others in our educator community. Not only are we listening to the happenings within our four walls but we are also learning from those around us in our school and educator community. I will just as readily run into a veteran teacher's room to ask a management question as I will to the brand-new teacher next door. Both have a unique experience and perspective that can help expand my own. I love the fresh eyes of new teachers as much as I love the calm, controlled demeanor of the thirty-year educator. I desire to have both qualities present in my teaching.

Listening intently allows us to further understand and adapt our classroom procedures and environments to meet students where they need us to be. If content understanding and exploration is our goal, then we need to understand how to best fit the needs of the students with whom we share the space. As you listen to the goings-on within the room and pinpoint potential ways to interject greatness, the next step is to address each moment by giving it your fullest attention. If there was a procedure missing, create a new routine to address it. If there were missing opportunities to help students, provide a way for those moments to take place. It is in these minute moments of thoughtful, purposeful reaction and adaptation that we truly amplify the current instruction. If we don't take time to really listen intently to what is really going on, these opportunities simply pass us by.

I'll tell you the time I am the best listener of all to everything happening in my room. It's when someone else walks in during a lesson. In those moments, my ears and posture perk up, and I am always amazed at how intently I can focus on every moment happening with an outsider in our midst. As the classroom guest wanders over to a group of students, I think I can even hear their breathing pattern. In those times, I think of all the ways I want things to run.

Rather than being reactive to the situation and getting frustrated if it isn't right, I dissect it to see what I can do to make it better. If you are reading this during summer or an off-teaching block, try to glean from those memories of moments in your own practice. What can you do to ensure that every group and every activity is at its fullest potential?

If you aren't the type to have a full daily class meeting, think of how you can have just a moment in your day to amplify a procedure, routine, or expectation with your students. I like to project an action shot up on the screen a couple of times a week. This is simply a picture I have taken on my phone during our instruction where kids are in action. These captured moments around the room are the easiest way to show students my expectations. To take these action shots, I will leave my small-group table for a few seconds and take a lap around the room. I listen to conversations, look at materials, notice student posture and positions, and generally get a feel for the level of engagement.

This routine of the surprise lap around the room is not meant as an evaluation or formal walk-through. Many times it is just a way to gather information solely for me. I don't draw attention to myself or try to stop and interject into what is already happening. If I do snap a photo or two, it usually goes unnoticed.

Later, as I look at these photos with my students, I begin to ask questions. What do the materials look like? How are students' bodies positioned? Students do not always have an understanding of how body position can increase learning. They also respond well to the visual of how materials are used and activities are accessed by seeing it done in a photo. Rather than talking about expectations, showing students doing the actual task and pinpointing discussions makes the conversation relevant and powerful.

For noise level, you can record a video or sound recording of students working to play back. These action shots taken a couple of times a week are used as a praise report. If you have student bodies or faces in the recording, it should be an affirmation of good habits, body language, effort, routine, materials handling, etc. It reinforces the habits, routines, and procedures I want while also encouraging students and letting them know their efforts are seen and acknowledged. This also allows students to see the desired expectation frequently while being uplifted for their efforts. Students feel seen. It keeps management at the front of the conversation.

We want students to be comfortable discussing these moments with each other in an open forum. That receptivity opens the door to also having them say things like "I want to be able to meet those expectations, but I am struggling with this part of the learning." These snapshots up on the screen make *everyone* feel like the magic happening during the math block is a result of each person's role in the room—because it is. Sometimes we talk about everything happening in order to allow that moment to happen. You can draw attention to anything you need to address.

FUELING FEEDBACK WITH THE THREE CS

To jump into the topic of feedback, I am going to share my "Three Cs" for fueling change in my classroom: conversations, checkpoints, and convey. These are just helpful ways to remember my purpose in feedback and to keep it in check for positive change. Feedback can be powerful. It can create instant and immense positive change, but unfortunately, it can also create instant and immense negative change. We've all had moments, as students, when a teacher's remark, written comment on work, or grade took the wind out of our sails and soured us toward the learning. Instead, let's highlight ways for positive feedback to happen.

Conversations might be the most effective and powerful way to transform classroom interactions for the better. Whatever the roadblock to the learning may be, having frequent conversations with students can keep lines of communication open and leave your students more receptive to accepting feedback. This doesn't need to be an added student conference schedule. That's asking a lot. Rather, conversations should result from a more natural effort to reach out to students, asking a question about their lives that we know can create a conversation.

Conversations don't always need to be weighty. If students know that you care about them when they aren't having an issue, they will not be quite so adversarial when it's time to give feedback on something academic. You can begin by simply taking note of something that's not too personal. Even just noticing something that makes a student smile or laugh can be noted for a future way to start a conversation. In order to make sure everyone gets some attention and conversation time, keep a little class list and mark off students you've chatted with over a week's time. A conversation on the way to the cafeteria, at recess, in between periods, as you pack up and wait to dismiss, etc. Anywhere it can fit! These small moments will amplify the way to harder conversations that will need to happen occasionally.

Checkpoints can be built into our reflection in order to close up the lesson on certain days or even situated as part of the warm-up as we open our math block for the day. The purpose of a checkpoint is to promote thinking in an area of our day or, in this case, in our math block. There are so many integral facets to the math block hour that our checkpoints can range from routines to social interactions to accountability to academics. A checkpoint on any of these topics allows students to state how they believe things are going, where they fit in in a spectrum of expectations, and how it could improve. Checkpoints should be specific as well as goal focused. The main focus is on improvement, reteaching, or highlighting positive traits for a desired habit or quality. Checkpoints are quick and purposeful.

Checkpoints should be timely and useful in order to be effective; they shouldn't be done if they aren't needed, but waiting to address an issue because you didn't have time that day when it rose to your attention will make the checkpoint less effective. Try to be flexible and open to adding checkpoints to a closing reflection if the need arises. Sometimes something happens that can't be addressed that day. For this, I open our next math block with the issue in a meeting in order to show students the importance of the matter.

Finally, it's crucial that feedback is purposeful; it's meant to convey a clear idea. Sometimes we don't realize that while trying to improve something, we actually create a negative interaction. Don't follow my mistakes of turning a checkpoint into an entire lesson about a specific problem. Instead, convey how group one is really keeping things clean and tidy. Post a picture up on the screen and thank them. Ask the members of that group how they decide who does what and how they are able to do it so quickly and consistently. Then, privately and personally address issues with groups or individuals who need to improve. We want to convey positive traits, great habits, and student strengths. All of this should be goal focused.

Be careful to avoid making feedback feel like a competition between students or groups to be better or the best, and try not to hold students to standards that are too strict or controlling or that are not realistic or sustainable. If students feel so closely monitored and are being told they don't measure up, it's easy to start a negative feedback cycle. Continue conversations, have needed checkpoints highlighting positive traits and promoting thinking in that direction, and convey great traits and habits of everyone. Use that checklist to be sure that all students are recognized as having a great habit, trait, or strength.

PRAISING THE THREE ES

Part of amplifying our math block means practicing praise. Praise is a powerful and motivating tool in transforming student response that, when compared to other instructional practices, does not require much effort to implement. As we know, praise indicates teacher approval while providing insight into current expectations. Just like we can shape our instruction to be more effective, we can also shape how we praise students for maximum outcomes.

There are three main areas to consider for praise, and I call them the "Three Es": effort, engagement, and enthusiasm. Each of these three areas of recognition, if praised correctly, can encourage a growth mindset, leading to priceless potential. We've all been guilty of the lazy man's praise track: good job, nice work, you tried your best, etc. Let's put an end to empty praise here and now. It can derail progress and reinforce minimal student effort. Students who earn an "atta boy" for minimal effort are likely to believe that the teacher has a low set of expectations or that the teacher thinks this is the best they can do.

Praising student effort means looking for the type of effort that sets out a student above their current track. It's not an "effort competition" from student to student. Instead, praising effort is actually an individualized and private act. When looking at student effort, look for that extra and above effort—not just work for work's sake but an effort that shows growth. Knowing students in the small-group setting will help you notice this effort easily. You'll know students' math minds, strategies, strengths, and effort level because of the time you've spent with them in close proximity. If a student that generally struggles with something that others do not takes on the challenge to push to overcome this concept, we want to notice and build up that effort through specific and private praise. Depending on the age of the student, a kind word, note, or even short conversation can validate the student to the point of impacting future confidence and trust in working through hard concepts as they are encountered through the school year. The key to praising effort is to keep the praise about the effort and not the achievement. The achievement is merely the outcome of the desired behavior. Sometimes effort brings achievement, but many times it does not.

Like effort, we want to pinpoint and praise exceptional examples of student engagement that furthers the potential for learning. Engagement is being "all in" on the task at hand. Engagement can be many things. It can mean highlighting exceptional qualities of stamina when a student approaches a given task. Or when students model the appropriate roles within a partner or group activity that keeps the activity on track and useful for all involved. Engagement in full-body response to transitions, callbacks, and interactive lessons. Giving specific, meaningful, and timely praise for student engagement reinforces this desired behavior throughout the year. There's a fine line on praising exceptional engagement publicly and privately. If the effort has helped the group and you know the group can also appreciate and praise the engagement, I would most definitely make it a public praise report. However, if the student is a private person who has performed this engagement outside of their comfort zone, publicly drawing more attention to it may deter them from future efforts. Being aware of the student's personality and the situation will lead us to lavishly praise in the way that is best.

Finally, we want to praise enthusiasm! Enthusiasm is a counterpart to both effort and engagement. Math can be exhilarating, but it is also challenging. Attitude can pull us out of a frustrated mindset. A frustrated mindset is going to happen in a math classroom. The very nature of math is a constant stream of different types of problems that we must solve. It is important to highlight that we can take on challenging tasks with enthusiasm and a positive attitude. Again, we don't praise the achievement but rather the positive attitude that was the catalyst to the achievement. Enthusiasm begets a mind shift from "This is going to be hard for me, and I am not sure how I will get through it" to "I am up for a hard challenge today!"

The AMPED math block makes it a priority to notice and value student effort, engagement, and enthusiasm. We recognize that many math tasks require students to work hard and put forth considerable effort without seeing immediate results. Recognizing any part of that process boosts morale, let's students know you notice and believe in their efforts, and encourages continued efforts to reach goals.

CHAPTER 6

DEVELOPMENT:
EMPOWERED
MATHEMATICIANS

As you develop, implement, and iterate your AMPED math block, you'll start to see surprising changes, in both yourself and your students. These transformations won't be magic, and they won't happen overnight, but they will become a natural outcome of the attentive, intentional, and empathic habits you'll be putting into practice each and every day. As the school year rolls on, it's important not to squander these changes or take them for granted. Instead, take the time to honor, appreciate, and then *amplify* the incredible strides you and your students are making.

In this chapter, we'll explore several key ways you can recognize your students' successes while still pushing your mathematicians even further. Growth, after all, is an endless process, and you'll want to ensure that your students have plenty of opportunities not just to *meet* expectations but to *exceed* them in dazzling ways.

LEANING INTO STUDENT LEADERSHIP

My first attempts at the guided math structure were in the early 2000s with primary-grade students. At that time, I was experimenting with how to run the structure and manage almost thirty six-year-old students as I sent them off to do independent activities. As you may imagine, my release was controlled and gradual. I began with just one station on Fridays. We looked forward to this all week, and I held it over them as much as I could. Shame on me, I know—using math as both a reward and a threat to good behavior.

As we took part in math workstations, my students and I became more confident and comfortable in what we were doing and why we were doing it. However, if I could graph the successful on-task minutes my first few years, the graph would look like a never-ending, death-defying roller coaster. Plenty of highs only to be sent screaming down lower than I began. Quite a few loops and twists. A few moments where we shot out at the speed of light, only to come to a screeching halt before a big goal. When the after-ride photos came out, there was a range of screaming with both arms raised, holding on for our lives in terror, or simply crying tears of hysterical laughter. I think that covers the experience.

During this time and especially with this age group, I was desperate for ways to help students know what to do to be successful. I noticed that I would always have at least one student that knew everyone's business on the computer. So, I would appoint that student as the computer expert. Don't know your password? Just ask Techie Treyvon. Need help cleaning up? Samara Sorts-a-Lot would love to lend a hand. Slowly but surely, I began to take note of personality and leadership qualities that would be helpful for our launch into this new way of conducting math.

When I was tied up with learning moments in small groups, I needed these capable students to be the go-betweens. Depending on the age group of my students, I would call these students different things: leaders, study buddies, class helpers, their highnesses . . . I wasn't too picky. I was desperate for student leadership.

I realized each year, as my classroom filled with new students, that I always had a few who had natural leadership qualities. With older students, I would create an application for students and make very clear my expectations about how successful applicants should help others correctly. With younger students, designating leaders was as simple as a fun name necklace that said, for example, "Study Buddy." It's important to note that students who do not care for the role should not be pushed into it or expected to uphold it. Student leaders need to be those who want the role and enjoy fulfilling it. But what I found is that while some students naturally possess leadership qualities, they have no desire to use them. Other students will emerge who will, with challenge and coaching, fill a desired classroom role. In any case, we want what is best for the entire classroom environment. So, whether a student innately loves the role or they find themselves appointed into it by the longings of their classmates, these leadership roles are part of what makes AMPED guided math successful.

Whether they are six years old or sixteen years old, students respond the same way to special attention. With time, then, I also learned how to uphold leaders with high esteem, pouring enthusiasm and high praise into these crucial classroom crusaders. Having a special lunch meeting while praising them for giving tips and lessening interruptions was one way to keep morale high so I could continue to depend on these willing students.

The ultimate goal in forming leadership roles is to model and uphold the standard of your best routines, procedures, and outcomes. We want this for every lesson and every student, but we have to begin with what naturally emerges during our initial launch phase and work outward from there. Notice students imitating leaders or motivated to be like those around them and nurture those new habits to their fullest potential. Call attention to those moments. Then, to keep the expectations and motivation high with the leadership team, guide students to reflect on class helpers and incorporate those moments into the class discussions and action shots.

IGNITING INDEPENDENCE

The topics of independence and accountability come up in workshops almost as much as the need for time. Through my experiences, both in my own classroom and in mentoring others in many grade levels, I've taken notice of two main things. First, all classes can improve their level of independence and quality of work with the help of some attributing factors. Second, the grade level does not determine the students' level of independence.

Every class has its challenges in both the quality of work and students' independence performing tasks. We can't control the maturity or academic levels of the students who appear on our class roster each school year. We do, however, have the ability to expose and shape those minds while they are within our four walls. Creating a classroom culture of independence and accountability is an ongoing process. We can be a huge catalyst in helping students understand and use the social and academic skills required with these traits, but we cannot introduce these ideals to students on Monday and expect that by Tuesday afternoon our room will be autonomous. It's important to recognize partial progress in all individuals and find joy in the process of working toward independence. The alternative is to focus on the unmet expectations that pit you against your students and leave you both frustrated. Some students are intrinsically capable of self-pacing and self-managing but many are not.

The best way to create an autonomous environment is to make the experience something joyful or meaningful for everyone that you work with little by little each day. When you find there is a breakdown in independence or on-task behavior, analyze the experience, scaffold it into milestones in the form of modeled steps, and practice each one. Explain each part of the desired routine in parts and work on it each day, each time providing as much positivity about it as you can muster. If students feel they are empowered and successful while carrying out a routine, they will continue it. Human nature is to want to be seen, heard, and understood. We can meet students where they are and encourage and push them to take little steps toward that big independent goal. When students are recognized for embodying desired traits, they feel seen and validated.

For kindergarteners or younger students, cultivating independence means teaching students how to handle a moment of misunderstanding without whining or crying or the need for you to get up. That's as big of a hurdle as keeping older students focused and on task when they want to just zone out during a workstation. Each age group has its challenges. Whatever the grade level, think of a creative, small goal to model and make it as fun as you can. If we bring light to whiny or off-task tendencies and explain that sometimes students get in their own way, we can dangle a carrot for them to push to a new level of independence.

Attaching meaning to goals is a great way to amplify results. If we desire independent behavior from students, we need to integrate meaningful goals into their daily math block experience and promote desired behavior. For example, when children are able to complete an activity and check in with a study buddy within the allotted time, the result is something meaningful or desirable for students that also continues to build independence. Maybe students unlock the privilege of a learning game with extra time. This allows students to have fun while still working independently.

Not only can we work on undesired behavior tendencies throughout the year, but what's really exciting is that we have the power to ignite independence in ways that really amplify the students' learning experience. If we are longing for more account-ability, we can think about the interactions we want to introduce to partners or groups that would create powerful moments of both collaboration and accountability. As the semester rolls on, I begin to ask myself important questions that will develop my students: What kind of check-ins can I create for individuals, partners, and groups? How can I create experiences to strengthen and bond my students in positive and growth-minded ways? What opportunities with people other than me can reinforce new healthy habits for teacher-dependent students?

CONCLUSION

KEEPING THE CURRENT

With this last section of the book, I want to highlight some key points on the topic of producing the high-yield gains of the AMPED guided math block. Through the last two decades of teaching mathematics, I have worked to amplify three areas: student learning, classroom culture, and classroom relationships. My initial implementation of the guided math structure was a paramount shift in the return on my mathematics investments, but within that structure, I discovered powerful, small moments of greater impact to further amplify these three areas year after year.

The first area of high yield that we need to be mindful of is producing the highest quantity of learning from each student within our school year. From the first week's benchmark assessment to the final exam or cumulative assessment, how have we ensured high-yield returns? So much goes into student learning, but many times we find ourselves in intricate discussions about how the adopted curriculum doesn't cover a certain aspect of the instruction as well as another program. While resources do play a role in learning, we directly control the content being worked on in our room. When creating the formula for student learning, it is our role to consider the content or skills we will cover, the resources provided for doing so, and most importantly, the students' mathematical needs.

The guided math structure allows us a front-row seat to the learning happening daily. We instruct the whole group in a mini-lesson, then we monitor and assess in close proximity to our mathematicians as they explore the concepts in a small group. We learn to look for the stages of mathematical understanding as we also gain insight into each student's patterns for problem-solving, strategies for attacking problems, and daily mathematical practices. In short, we gain access to the most powerful way to impact instruction: the student's math mind.

As we gain access to the math minds of our students, our instruction naturally begins to shift to meet those needs. This process continues to ensure that we drive instruction to meet students' needs, choosing content over resources. While resources are a helpful guide, they do not impact instruction. They simply provide the framework for a grade-level specific standards. *We* impact instruction by knowing our students' math minds.

REVISING CURRICULUM

Engineering a successful, AMPED math block is a process that never ends. The cycle of revising lesson plans for higher-yield learning can be modeled in much the same way as a high-stakes business-growth action plan: What am I trying to promote? Who is my target audience? What cues will my target audience respond favorably to? How can I present this in the best way possible for my target audience? Simply replace *target audience* with *students* and we have our instructional plan. When we create the instruction for learning, we consider our students' math minds above all and build from there.

Even with the guided math curriculum I designed myself, I would not teach it exactly as I designed it year after year. Curriculum is simply a framework to use to help plan instruction. While designing instructional materials, the standards are used to ensure high-quality content, but the use of the materials depends on knowing the developmental levels and abilities of the students in that instructional year. This is one reason there is never going to be a perfect adopted curriculum: what one teacher finds exceptional another may find lacking. The real students in my classroom are the driving force in planning any and all instruction.

In the same way, what worked wonderfully this year will still need to be adjusted for next year's learners. Teaching is so much more than speaking the same lessons to students year after year. It is layers upon layers of factors from environment, learning styles, purpose, focus, personalities, laws and guidelines, experiences, and oh right . . . students and resources. It's no wonder we are tired and overwhelmed. It's easy to lose focus with all of the pressures we experience.

We do our best to create the best experience for our students as we navigate through all of these factors daily. That's the key to keeping your joy. How can I create the best experience for these individuals right now? One that excites me to teach while empowering them to be their best possible self as they learn. Keeping focused on the learners in the room and having a teaching-is-my-mission attitude has always helped remind me why I do this.

You likely picked up this book with the idea that you could change something about your current math instruction. For me it began as a brand-new teacher standing at the front of the room with my scripted math program. My heart bursting with anticipation as I had finally reached the level of being the expert mathematician in the room. Although this was a moment I had often considered and anticipated during my training, the result was nothing like I had expected.

It was finally my time to use the math manipulatives and tools as my students watched intently. My joy and excitement for the moment was not translating to a roomful of eager mathematicians. In that moment, with twenty-five pairs of eyes lacking excitement or joy looking at me, I silently vowed that I would change how I taught math. I wanted *every* student to be the expert mathematician in the room with access to all of the tools, manipulatives, and experiences that would create a joy and excitement for solving math problems.

No one has a perfect math block from beginning to end day after day. Allow grace for yourself and your students. Humans are messy, multifaceted, and magnificent. Orchestrating a roomful of students as they acquire a love and a deep understanding of math is an incredible feat! When there is a breakdown, a behavior problem, or a bombed lesson, you are still doing it right. Rather than taking those moments personally or becoming discouraged by them, simply take the opportunity to apply the AMPED instructional areas as needed.

As you move forward in designing the AMPED guided math block, remember this process builds over time in small meaningful moments. Take one goal and carefully follow the AMPED instructional practices to make the most of the lesson experience. Once you have the first goal working well, add the next goal. Over time, the desired environment, lesson delivery outcomes, and student-centered learning experiences will all become comfortable and even second nature.

As you develop, implement, and iterate your AMPED math block, you'll start to see surprising changes, in both yourself and your students. These transformations won't be magic, and they won't happen overnight, but they will become a natural outcome of the attentive, intentional, and empathic habits you'll be putting into practice each and every day.

Rather than becoming complacent with less than desirable results, the AMPED process will invigorate both the teacher and students. The idea that every moment in our math block can be amped by our purposeful planning allows teachers to design and carry out a targeted and impactful learning experience. The art and gift of the profession of teacher or educator is not to simply follow any adopted curriculum without the consideration of the pupils. AMPED math instruction allows each professional to personally consider all factors of the math block for the best possible results over a career of meaningful math moments.

NOTES

Johnson, Emma. "What Is the Concrete Pictorial Abstract (CPA) Approach and How to Use It in Maths." Third Space Learning. December 10, 2020. https://thirdspacelearning.com/blog/concrete-pictorial-abstract-maths-cpa/.

Newton, Nicki. "Developing Mathematical Proficiency in Guided Math Groups." Dr. Nicki's Guided Math Blog. September 25, 2010. https://guidedmath.wordpress.com/2010/09/25/developing-mathematical-proficiency-in-guided-math-groups/.

Sammons, Laney. *Guided Math: A Framework for Mathematics Instruction*. Huntington Beach, CA: Shell Education, 2009.

ACKNOWLEDGMENTS

To Kristina Grant: Your whole-hearted belief in and honesty about *Guided Math* throughout our teaching careers and friendship has changed how the message of *Guided Math* meets the ears and eyes of educators. I am so grateful for the hours upon hours spent reading, researching, discussing, experimenting, writing, revising, designing, and more to make *Guided Math* what it is in every facet. Having a best friend and teaching partner who cares about every math moment just as much as I do is a true blessing and gift. Thank you for your unmatched interest and support of all things *Guided Math*. From spoken words after school to a full-blown partnership in business, I am forever grateful for you.

To Lindsey and the Reading List: You have been an incredible source of help through the entire process of this book. The incredible attention and expertise you have applied to the words on these pages is greatly appreciated. I am humbled at the creativity, artistry, and understanding of the message through every beautifully edited word within these pages.

To Dave and Shelley Burgess: Thank you for supporting my dream of writing this book and for valuing the ideas of every educator.

To Tara Martin: Thank you for being the champion encourager and supporter to the ideas, thoughts, and experiences across education and especially within the pages of this book.

To the supporters and endorsers of this book: Thank you for the interest and enthusiasm for sharing the message of magnifying math moments through this book. Your support and encouragement made this book a reality.

To the readers of this book: Thank you for taking a chance on yourself and your students by picking up this book. I am honored that you believe in me and have allowed me to share my favorite math moments with you.

ABOUT THE AUTHOR

REAGAN TUNSTALL incorporates twenty-two years of teaching experience into her idea-packed workshops. Reagan's passion for teaching, combined with her training experience, drives her to share the effectiveness of developing a community of empowered mathematical thinkers in the classroom and leaves teachers revitalized and eager to implement her ideas. She has led districts in the implementation of the math standards through guided math practices. Reagan has authored over one thousand teaching resources including *Guided Math*, a math program used in hundreds of districts across the US. Reagan writes at Tunstall's Teaching Tidbits while working as an educational consultant, speaker, and author.

BRING REAGAN TUNSTALL TO YOUR SCHOOL, EVENT, OR ORGANIZATION

CONNECT WITH REAGAN TUNSTALL

🌐 tunstallsteachingtidbits.com

✉ reagan.tunstall@gmail.com

Teachers pay Teachers:
teacherspayteachers.com/store/Reagan-Tunstall

f reagtunstall

@reagtunstall

@reagantunstall

youtube.com/user/reagantunstall

Reagan Tunstall

MORE FROM

Since 2012, DBCI has published books that inspire and equip educators to be their best. For more information on our titles or to purchase bulk orders for your school, district, or book study, visit **DaveBurgessConsulting.com/DBCIbooks**.

MORE FROM THE *LIKE A PIRATE*™ SERIES

Teach Like a PIRATE by Dave Burgess

eXPlore Like a PIRATE by Michael Matera

Learn Like a PIRATE by Paul Solarz

Play Like a PIRATE by Quinn Rollins

Run Like a PIRATE by Adam Welcome

Tech Like a PIRATE by Matt Miller

LEAD LIKE A PIRATE™ SERIES

Lead Like a PIRATE by Shelley Burgess and Beth Houf

Balance Like a PIRATE by Jessica Cabeen, Jessica Johnson, and Sarah Johnson

Lead beyond Your Title by Nili Bartley

Lead with Appreciation by Amber Teamann and Melinda Miller

Lead with Culture by Jay Billy

Lead with Instructional Rounds by Vicki Wilson

Lead with Literacy by Mandy Ellis

LEADERSHIP & SCHOOL CULTURE

Culturize by Jimmy Casas

Escaping the School Leader's Dunk Tank by Rebecca Coda and Rick Jetter

Fight Song by Kim Bearden

From Teacher to Leader by Starr Sackstein

If the Dance Floor Is Empty, Change the Song by Joe Clark

The Innovator's Mindset by George Couros

It's OK to Say "They" by Christy Whittlesey

Kids Deserve It! by Todd Nesloney and Adam Welcome

Let Them Speak by Rebecca Coda and Rick Jetter

The Limitless School by Abe Hege and Adam Dovico

Live Your Excellence by Jimmy Casas

Next-Level Teaching by Jonathan Alsheimer

The Pepper Effect by Sean Gaillard

Principaled by Kate Barker, Kourtney Ferrua, and Rachael George

The Principled Principal by Jeffrey Zoul and Anthony McConnell

Relentless by Hamish Brewer

The Secret Solution by Todd Whitaker, Sam Miller, and Ryan Donlan

Start. Right. Now. by Todd Whitaker, Jeffrey Zoul, and Jimmy Casas

Stop. Right. Now. by Jimmy Casas and Jeffrey Zoul

Teachers Deserve It by Rae Hughart and Adam Welcome

Teach Your Class Off by CJ Reynolds

They Call Me "Mr. De" by Frank DeAngelis

Thrive through the Five by Jill M. Siler

Unmapped Potential by Julie Hasson and Missy Lennard

When Kids Lead by Todd Nesloney and Adam Dovico

Word Shift by Joy Kirr

Your School Rocks by Ryan McLane and Eric Lowe

TECHNOLOGY & TOOLS

50 Things You Can Do with Google Classroom by Alice Keeler and Libbi Miller

50 Things to Go Further with Google Classroom by Alice Keeler and Libbi Miller

140 Twitter Tips for Educators by Brad Currie, Billy Krakower, and Scott Rocco

Block Breaker by Brian Aspinall

Building Blocks for Tiny Techies by Jamila "Mia" Leonard

Code Breaker by Brian Aspinall

The Complete EdTech Coach by Katherine Goyette and Adam Juarez

Control Alt Achieve by Eric Curts

The Esports Education Playbook by Chris Aviles, Steve Isaacs, Christine Lion-Bailey, and Jesse Lubinsky

Google Apps for Littles by Christine Pinto and Alice Keeler

Master the Media by Julie Smith

Reality Bytes by Christine Lion-Bailey, Jesse Lubinsky, and Micah Shippee, PhD

Sail the 7 Cs with Microsoft Education by Becky Keene and Kathi Kersznowski

Shake Up Learning by Kasey Bell

Social LEADia by Jennifer Casa-Todd

Stepping Up to Google Classroom by Alice Keeler and Kimberly Mattina

Teaching Math with Google Apps by Alice Keeler and Diana Herrington

Teachingland by Amanda Fox and Mary Ellen Weeks

TEACHING METHODS & MATERIALS

All 4s and 5s by Andrew Sharos

Boredom Busters by Katie Powell

The Classroom Chef by John Stevens and Matt Vaudrey

The Collaborative Classroom by Trevor Muir

Copyrighteous by Diana Gill

CREATE by Bethany J. Petty

Ditch That Homework by Matt Miller and Alice Keeler

Ditch That Textbook by Matt Miller

Don't Ditch That Tech by Matt Miller, Nate Ridgway, and Angelia Ridgway

EDrenaline Rush by John Meehan

Educated by Design by Michael Cohen, The Tech Rabbi

The EduProtocol Field Guide by Marlena Hebern and
  Jon Corippo

The EduProtocol Field Guide: Book 2 by Marlena Hebern and
  Jon Corippo

The EduProtocol Field Guide: Math Edition by Lisa Nowakowski
  and Jeremiah Ruesch

Game On? Brain On! by Lindsay Portnoy, PhD

Innovating Play by Jessica LaBar-Twomy and Christine Pinto

Instant Relevance by Denis Sheeran

LAUNCH by John Spencer and A.J. Juliani

Make Learning MAGICAL by Tisha Richmond

Pass the Baton by Kathryn Finch and Theresa Hoover

Project-Based Learning Anywhere by Lori Elliott

Pure Genius by Don Wettrick

The Revolution by Darren Ellwein and Derek McCoy

Shift This! by Joy Kirr

Skyrocket Your Teacher Coaching by Michael Cary Sonbert

Spark Learning by Ramsey Musallam

Sparks in the Dark by Travis Crowder and Todd Nesloney

Table Talk Math by John Stevens

Unpack Your Impact by Naomi O'Brien and LaNesha Tabb

The Wild Card by Hope and Wade King

The Writing on the Classroom Wall by Steve Wyborney

INSPIRATION, PROFESSIONAL GROWTH & PERSONAL DEVELOPMENT

Be REAL by Tara Martin

Be the One for Kids by Ryan Sheehy

The Coach ADVenture by Amy Illingworth

Creatively Productive by Lisa Johnson

Educational Eye Exam by Alicia Ray

The EduNinja Mindset by Jennifer Burdis

Empower Our Girls by Lynmara Colón and Adam Welcome

Finding Lifelines by Andrew Grieve and Andrew Sharos

The Four O'Clock Faculty by Rich Czyz

How Much Water Do We Have? by Pete and Kris Nunweiler

P Is for Pirate by Dave and Shelley Burgess

A Passion for Kindness by Tamara Letter

The Path to Serendipity by Allyson Apsey

Sanctuaries by Dan Tricarico

Saving Sycamore by Molly B. Hudgens

The SECRET SAUCE by Rich Czyz

Shattering the Perfect Teacher Myth by Aaron Hogan

Stories from Webb by Todd Nesloney

Talk to Me by Kim Bearden

Teach Better by Chad Ostrowski, Tiffany Ott, Rae Hughart, and Jeff Gargas

Teach Me, Teacher by Jacob Chastain

Teach, Play, Learn! by Adam Peterson

The Teachers of Oz by Herbie Raad and Nathan Lang-Raad

TeamMakers by Laura Robb and Evan Robb

Through the Lens of Serendipity by Allyson Apsey

The Zen Teacher by Dan Tricarico

CHILDREN'S BOOKS

Beyond Us by Aaron Polansky

Cannonball In by Tara Martin

Dolphins in Trees by Aaron Polansky

I Want to Be a Lot by Ashley Savage

The Princes of Serendip by Allyson Apsey

Ride with Emilio by Richard Nares

The Wild Card Kids by Hope and Wade King

Zom-Be a Design Thinker by Amanda Fox

Made in the USA
Monee, IL
10 July 2023